Women in the Church, St. Catherine of Siena, Fr. Teilhard de Chardin, & Criminal Reformation

By
David H. Lukenbill

A Chulu Press Book

Chulu Press First Edition published 2014

IBSN: 978-0-9892429-1-2

Published by The Lampstand Foundation

We glorify God to attract others to Him; through the Catholic Gate to the Mystical Church

For Marlene & Erika Always

Contents

Preface

This is the ninth book in our annual book publication schedule, which, along with our annual policy papers, forms the foundation of our apostolate work at the Lampstand Foundation.

As my ultimate audience, beyond the members of Lampstand, are penitential criminals, many of whom are in prison. Consequently, my books are written by marshaling various resources through copious quotes to help make the points I am attempting to get across; and these are to important for my penitential criminal/prisoner audience who have little access to research libraries or the internet.

I remember, while in prison, reading books whose ideas were subtle and not easily understood, cutting against the grain of the norm I was familiar with; books that were often largely narrative with few references, which would raise the question, how does the author know that? And with no access to academic libraries to seek out support of the position taken, I could easily discount it as one author's opinion.

Consequently, I use a lot of references for my ideas, and for those readers in prison who have little access to research, creating enough of a narrative to provide support.

For this book, a quote from Groppe (2009) frames the over-arching theme:

In a culture that systematically denigrates, commodifies, and violates women's bodies in advertising, film, and pornography, it is imperative that the church bear public and symbolic witness to the mystery that women and men alike can serve as an icon of Wisdom made flesh. (p. 171)

That is bare bone essence, isn't it?

The Church stands in the world as a sign of contradiction and as the world since time immemorial excluded women from full personhood; the Church *must* ensure that within her embrace, woman's full personhood is deeply rooted and complete; which can only be accomplished by priestly ordination and full equality with men in the leadership of the Church on earth as that equality is certainly so in Heaven.

I have come to believe, fully and completely, that the institutional Church has been wrong in not ordaining women to be priests; just as the Church was wrong for centuries in seeing the earth as the center of the solar system, and slavery as acceptable and usury not; and this wrongness, in the treatment of women, will become obvious to criminals being evangelized, for they know, better than most, the pain and sorrow of being marginalized, even though their marginalization is self-imposed while that of the women in the Church comes from the Vatican and twisted history.

Underneath and alongside the institutional church, the deeper reality of the supernatural church has always existed, the Church founded and shaped by Christ, the Church the people in their hearts have always seen—for the institutional church has too much that has been claimed as doctrine, then changed—but the supernatural church, the mystical church, has always known the true and equal power of the women in the Church.

My Catholic belief is centered on the Great Story; that throughout human history the idea of God has been prevalent within the human heart and mind; and of the four major religions: Christianity, Islam, Hinduism, Buddhism, only three, Christianity, Islam, and Buddhism can claim an individual as founder, and of them only one, Christianity, can claim a founder who was God; the other two merely claiming to be prophet and enlightened respectively.

Christ's Godhood is certified by eye witness accounts of miracles he performed unexplainable by any human ability; in particular, his resurrection.

Christ formed his church on the rock of Peter, and the gates of hell have not prevailed against it, and as the Roman Catholic Church survives still, I know that, as a Catholic, I am of the People of God, and I am as certain that God is in the soul of each human being on earth.

"Question Authority"; that was the foundational mantra of the 1960s; choosing to question the authority that was instructing them to do something they felt was wrong and incorrect teaching is, unfortunately, an aspect of Catholic institutional life; but it is corrected by the Catholic teaching mandating listening to one's conscience, as *Gaudium et Spes* (1965) teaches us:

> **16.** In the depths of his conscience, man detects a law which he does not impose upon himself, but which holds him to obedience. Always summoning

him to love good and avoid evil, the voice of conscience when necessary speaks to his heart: do this, shun that. For man has in his heart a law written by God; to obey it is the very dignity of man; according to it he will be judged.

This comes from the point made in Romans 2:14-16:

> **14** When Gentiles who have not the law do by nature what the law requires, they are a law to themselves, even though they do not have the law. **15** They show that what the law requires is written on their hearts, while their conscience also bears witness and their conflicting thoughts accuse or perhaps excuse them **16** on that day when, according to my gospel, God judges the secrets of men by Christ Jesus.

All human beings have the eternal written on their hearts and even within those who do not believe in God, even some who call themselves Humanists, as is evident when the father of Humanism, Abraham Maslow (1971) writes about the first step to the supreme heights a human being can reach, that of self-actualization:

> As a simple first step toward self-actualization, I sometimes suggest to my students that when they a given a glass of wine and asked how they like it, they try a different way of responding. First, I suggest that they *not* look at the label on the bottle. Thus they will not use it to get any cue about whether or not they *should* like it. Next, I recommend that they close their eyes if possible and that they "make a hush." Now they are ready to look within themselves and try to shut out the noise

of the world so that they may savor the wine on their tongues and look to the "Supreme Court" inside themselves. Then, and only then, they may come out and say, "I like it" or I don't like it." (p. 46)

This "Supreme Court" is conscience, the ability to determine right from wrong or even good wine from bad wine, according to taste, the taste of a well-informed conscience, or, of listening, in that quietness, that "hush" , which, as Christians call it, the still small voice, which, when heeded, serves us well.

Catholic teaching is absolutely correct, one's conscience, one's connection with God, is surely what one must align with, which calls for the attitude, "trust but verify" and verify through our own study, our own conscience, our own listening to that still small voice from God, our own entering into the hush.

Catherine of Siena (1980) captures this elegantly, in *The Dialogue*, God is the speaker:

> Imagine a circle traced on the ground, and in its center a tree sprouting with a shoot grafted into its side. The tree finds its nourishment in the soil within the expanse of the circle, but uprooted from the soil it would die fruitless. So think of the soul as a tree made for love and living only by love. Indeed, without this divine love, which is true and perfect charity, death would be her fruit instead of life. The circle in which this tree's root, the soul's love, must grow is true knowledge of herself, knowledge that is joined to me, who like the circle have neither beginning nor end. You can go round and round

within this circle, finding neither end nor beginning, yet never leaving the circle. This knowledge of yourself, and of me within yourself, is grounded in the soil of true humility, which is as great as the expanse of the circle (which is the knowledge of yourself united with me, as I have said). But if your knowledge of yourself were isolated from me there would be no full circle at all. Instead there would be a beginning in self-knowledge, but apart from me it would end in confusion. (pp. 41-42)

Introduction

I was born in 1942, to a German/Russian father and Jewish/English mother. My father soon was sentenced to prison for crimes committed as a member of an organized crime family and after a time, my mother remarried.

My stepfather was a Danish Mormon and I was raised—from 5 years old to 13—as a Mormon.

At 13 I committed my first theft and it was glorious. I became a criminal—thief and robber—and for the next 20 years plied my trade, not always successfully as I spent 12 of those years in jails, youth homes, reformatories (all of which I escaped from) and maximum security state and federal prisons, (from which I could not escape).

Later, after release in the waning days of the 1960s, I became a New Ager, and wandered drug-soaked, sensually gorged and joyful, among the glittering trappings of Gnosticism.

When I married and we had a child, we decided to explore religions to find a faith home for our family life and slowly rewound our way through Protestantism, Judaism, and Mormonism, until finally settling on Catholicism; being baptized in 2004.

At each step in my journey to the Catholic Church, I studied deeply the theology and praxis of the chosen faith and in each case, the theology came up short; except for

Catholicism, whose richness kept rewarding me the deeper I studied.

Even when I began a deep study of the dissenting theologians of the Church—as I have always believed in the role of the devil's advocate—I found much to confirm my Catholic faith; but less to confirm the institutional church.

Here is where I found myself, in the year 2013, when I began to realize that the true church was the Mystical Church; but the greatest gate to the Mystical Church was the Apostolic Gate, the gate of the apostles and the fathers and mothers of the Catholic Church.

The Mystical Church is the Church God created when he created us; it is the way of life we know, in our God infused souls, that we should live by.

Human souls have directly communicated with God since the beginning and though they have often misunderstood God, or chosen to ignore or go against God, they have known what God wants them to do, how God wants then to live their lives on earth.

This is the Mystical Church

The Mystical Church is the church Christ—God become man—enhanced upon the earth two thousand years ago in Israel.

He was born on earth as a member of the chosen people of God, from a Jewish woman, impregnated by God.

He was the Messiah foretold in Jewish history and the Mystical Church created by him embraced and enhanced

Judaism, opening the Apostolic Gate to the Catholic Church.

Today, the Mystical Church is the Church found scattered—as is the way of humans—throughout the thousands of humanly corrupted gates of divine light

It is not the humanly corrupted churches of Catholicism, Buddhism, Islam, Protestantism, Hinduism, or Judaism; but through the Apostolic Gate is the truest path to the Mystical Church, and through the Apostolic Gate the greatest light shines on God's words to humans.

The universe is the creation of God and it is in the human mind able to envision the universe and traverse it, that the divine image is to be found.

We are warmed by the abyss of the night sky because human eyes gaze back at us and it is our destiny, as we traverse space and time, to someday meet our created brothers and sisters and we will find creedal and familial congruence with others who will also pray:

> I believe in God, the Father Almighty, Creator of heaven and earth; and in Jesus Christ, His only Son, our Lord: Who was conceived by the Holy Spirit, born of the Virgin Mary; suffered under Pontius Pilate, was crucified, died and was buried. He descended into hell; the third day He rose again from the dead; He ascended into heaven, is seated at the right hand of God the Father Almighty; from thence He shall come to judge the living and the dead. I believe in the Holy Spirit, the Holy Catholic Church, the communion of Saints, the forgiveness

of sins, the resurrection of the body, and life everlasting. Amen.

We are now at the Apostolic Gate and the Holy Catholic Church is the Mystical Church. It is the Church that is Holy, uncorrupted by human sin, and it is here for us, has always been here for us, it cannot fall, nor can the evil of Satan tarnish it as he can tarnish the human institutional church.

It is here in the creed, in the writings of the Holy Fathers and the Holy Mothers of the Church; the Angelic Doctor, the great Catechisms of Trent and Vatican II, and the documents of Vatican II, perhaps the most sublime set of documents ever to come from the Church.

Truth is rationale, beautiful and harmonious. Faith is built on reason, logic and order. The rational mind of human beings can comprehend the ways of God, even if it is only the current Doctors of the Church like Saint Catherine of Siena and St. Thomas Aquinas, or a future Doctor of the Church—I am sure of it—Fr. Teilhard de Chardin, who can so comprehend at the deepest level and then, teach us.

Catherine reasoned with worldly powers through her mystical faith; Aquinas taught us that reason and faith are congruent; and Fr. Teilhard de Chardin taught us that the praxis emanating from their congruence is evolutionary.

With this richness of past doctrinal study at their command, I am saddened by the lack of reasonable discourse being used by the Church to combat women's ordination, and the seminal argument of the Church is found in the *Catechism* (1994):

1577 "Only a baptized man (*vir*) validly receives sacred ordination." The Lord Jesus chose men (*viri*) to form the college of the twelve apostles, and the apostles did the same when they chose collaborators to succeed them in their ministry. The college of bishops, with whom the priests are united in the priesthood, makes the college of the twelve an ever-present and ever-active reality until Christ's return. The Church recognizes herself to be bound by this choice made by the Lord himself. For this reason the ordination of women is not possible.

Of course, Jesus Christ also only chose Jews to be apostles, but that is not now, nor has it ever been, considered as another scripturally-based requirement; and even more cogent, Vatican II's *Lumen Gentium* (2013) teaches us, trumping the *Catechism*:

> There is no room in Christ and in the Church for inequality on the grounds of race, nationality, social status or sex; for 'there is neither Jew nor Greek, there is neither slave nor free, there is neither male nor female, for you are all one in Christ Jesus' (*Gal.* 3:28; cf. *Col.* 3:11)

What to do, what to do?

Our questions lead us to the Kingdom of Conscience, the house of self-knowledge infused with knowledge of God, but always study, study, life-long learning, and prayer, daily prayer, hourly prayer, continuous prayer, seek the truth of doctrine.

Other doctrinal study—preceding the *Catechism*—on the issue is commented on by Swidler & Swidler (1977):

The Vatican Declaration on women priests [*Inter Insigniores: On the Question Of Admission of Women to the Ministerial Priesthood*, Pope Paul VI, 1976] did not fall out of some abstract logical Roman world, nor did it result from discussions and actions of ordaining women by non-Roman Catholic Churches, nor even from the Women's Liberation Movement (though the latter two were contributory influences). Rather, it came as a response to the movement for full Christian personhood for all Catholics, women included, flowing from the creative thought and actions of Vatican II. The Council's notions of participation of the laity in all aspects of the life of the Church, of collegiality, of the Church as the People of God, naturally led women to seek full exercise of their gifts as first-class members of that Church, of that People. That logically meant some women would be expected to experience a call to the priesthood—and in a non-discriminatory Church they ought to be able to have that call tested and respond to it if found authentic. Thus it was long before the birth of the Women's Liberation Movement (e. 1969) or before Catholics were talking seriously to non-Catholics who ordained women that pioneer Catholic women and men began to raise the issue of women priests.

This question-raising began at least with the petition to the Preparatory Commission of the Second Vatican Council (which began in 1962) submitted by the Catholic laywoman, Gertrude Heinzelman, a Swiss lawyer and member of St. Joan's International Alliance, which in its 1963 and 1964 Conventions also petitioned the Council concerning women priests. About the same time a most thorough-going Catholic study of the question of women priests was completed by the Dutch Father Haye van der Meer, S.J., as his doctoral dissertation written under the direction of Karl Rahner SJ, in Austria. In 1963, this time in Peru, another Catholic study was published, by Father José Idigoras, S.J. By the end of Vatican II more and more journal articles began to appear; in 1967 Sister V.E. Hannon in England completed another book-length study of women priests, and in 1970 Ida Raming earned her doctorate of Catholic theology in Germany with her dissertation an analysis of the canon law mandating only male priests. All of these studies concluded in favor of women priests. By this time studies and articles began to appear with ever growing rapidity, as is outlined in the bibliographical essay in the present book.

As far off as India the Catholic Church's concern for women in official Church ministries, including deaconate and priesthood, could be found up to the eve of the Vatican Declaration: "The present situation, therefore, in which all women are excluded from her ministries, only because they are women, should be rectified. This step should be taken without hesitation because: a) theological research recognizes that no valid reasons can be given against the installation of women in lay ministries, nor against their ordination as deacons (whereas the admission of women to the presbyterate remains a matter of discussion). Even stronger:" In the new order which Christ has created, women share fully in all the aspects of his redemptive priesthood. This implies of necessity that women should also participate in the sacramental priestly ministry. And this in a periodical published by the Catholic Bishops Conference India which goes to all bishops, priests, religious and many Catholic laity of India. This issue was a special one on "Ministries In the Church," and was so enthusiastically received that it had to be reprinted. It was the result of many months of serious study on the part of various scholars and consultants of church groups, some of which were directed by a number of Catholic bishops of India in person or through representatives. Then the issue was distributed to all the Catholic bishops of the Far East. (n.p.)

Trasancos (2013) describes the power of reasoned discourse in her book on Stanley Jaki, distinguished priest and physicist who died in 2009:

Jaki did not insist on the distinction between "exact science" and "reasoned discourse" to distinguish science, but to emphasize the *power* of reasoned discourse as a brief, but necessary side note, there is a theological underpinning to this emphasis related to the doctrine of *imago Dei*, that man is made in the image of God. Scripture revealed that the Holy Trinity is an ordered procession. The Father generates the Son as a divine internal act of the intellect (which is why the Son is also called the Word or the Logos) and the Father and Son together as one substance spirate the Holy Spirit as a divine internal act of the will. Thus humans created with a rational soul also have intellect and will. (Kindle Location 346-356)

Solomon's prayer in the New American Bible (2011) says:

> 1 God of my ancestors, Lord of mercy, you who have made all things by your word
> 2 And in your wisdom have established humankind to rule the creatures produced by you,
> 3 And to govern the world in holiness and righteousness, and to render judgment in integrity of heart;

And in the illuminating notes:

> The author identifies Wisdom with the word of God just as he again identifies Wisdom with the spirit of God in v. 17. All three are alternate ways of expressing God's activity in relationship with the world and its inhabitants. (9:1-2) (p. 866)

Wisdom has long been associated with women and, as Reuther (2005) in writing about the great Christian mystic Julian of Norwich, even combining Christ with woman/wisdom:

> This faith in God's enduring love and kindness is expressed in her [Julian] combined fathering and mothering language for God: "Thus in our making God almighty is our kindly Father, and God all-Wisdom is our kindly Mother, with the love and goodness of the Holy Spirit, which is all one God, one lord." Julian brings mothering language into the Trinity by a recovery of female-personified Wisdom, identified with the second person of the Trinity as Mother... "Thus Jesus Christ who does good against evil is our very Mother. We have our being of him, where every ground of Motherhood

begins, with all the sweet keeping of love that endlessly follows. As truly as God is our Father so truly is God our Mother." (p. 189)

This is an important aspect of the women theologian's study of this issue and Fiorenza (1983) puts a bow on it:

> The earliest Jesus traditions perceive this God of gracious goodness in a woman's *Gestalt* as divine *Sophia* (wisdom). The very old saying "Sophia is justified [or vindicated] by all her children" (Luke 7:35), probably had its setting in Jesus's table community with tax collectors, prostitutes, and sinners, as well. The Sophia-God of Jesus recognizes all Israelites as her children and she is proven "right" by all of them. (p. 132)

Understanding this connection—for only seeing with the one eye of the male theologians and chroniclers of Church history is a form of self-blinding—is crucial as we make our way into the thicket of the women's ordination movement, as Groppe (2009) writes:

> According to Aquinas, the person of Christ is the second person of the triune God—the divine Word (John 1:1-5) or Wisdom (I Cor. 1:24)—who assumed a human nature in order to redeem humanity and lead us to eternal communion with God...
>
> As the very Wisdom of the incomprehensible God, the *persona* of Christ is neither male nor female in the constricted human sense of these terms. And, at the same time, as the divine Wisdom, the *persona* of Christ is the origin of the perfections of both male and female persons—whatever these may be—

for it was through Wisdom that the cosmos was created. (p. 170)

Ruether (1993) puts another bow on it, making the connection between woman as the lowly—lowest of the lowly:

> Women play an important role in this Gospel vision of the vindication of the lowly in God's new order. It is the women of the oppressed and marginalized groups who are often pictured as the representatives of the lowly. The dialogue at the well takes place with a Samaritan woman. A Syro-Phoenician woman is the prophetic seeker who forces Jesus to concede redemption of the Gentiles. Among the poor it is the widows who are the most destitute. Among the ritually unclean, it is the woman with the flow of blood who extorts healing for herself contrary to the law. Among the morally outcast, it is the prostitutes who are the furthest from righteousness. The role played by women of marginalized groups is an intrinsic part of the iconoclastic, messianic vision. It means that the women are the oppressed of the oppressed. They are the bottom of the present social hierarchy and hence are seen, in a special way, as the last who will be first in the Kingdom of God. (pp. 136-137)

Yes, prostitutes and criminals are the farthest from God, yet, as we see with the prostitute Saint Mary of Magdalene and the thief Saint Dismas, were among those closest to him.

Yes, the search for truth is endless and we know that what once seemed reasonable and true can become false, perhaps not any better exhibited than through the case of the great scientist Galileo, imprisoned for life by the Catholic Church for expressing a truth which the Church, at that time, reasonably denied.

Wikipedia describes:

> Galileo Galilei (15 February 1564 – 8 January 1642)...was an Italian physicist, mathematician, astronomer, and philosopher who played a major role in the scientific revolution. His achievements include improvements to the telescope and consequent astronomical observations and support for Copernicanism. Galileo has been called the "father of modern observational astronomy", the "father of modern physics", the "father of science", and "the Father of Modern Science"...

> Galileo's championing of heliocentrism was controversial within his lifetime, when most subscribed to either geocentrism or the Tychonic system. He met with opposition from astronomers, who doubted heliocentrism due to the absence of an observed stellar parallax. The matter was investigated by the Roman Inquisition in 1615, which concluded that heliocentrism was false and contrary to scripture, placing works advocating the Copernican system on the index of banned books and forbidding Galileo from advocating heliocentrism. Galileo later defended his views in *Dialogue Concerning the Two Chief World Systems*, which appeared to attack Pope Urban VIII and thus alienated him and the Jesuits, who had both supported Galileo up until this point. He was tried by the Holy Office, then found "vehemently

suspect of heresy", was forced to recant, and spent the rest of his life under house arrest. It was while Galileo was under house arrest that he wrote one of his finest works, *Two New Sciences*, in which he summarised the work he had done some forty years earlier, on the two sciences now called kinematics and strength of materials. (n.p.)

Retrieved February 9, 2014 from http://en.wikipedia.org/wiki/Galileo_Galilei

It was reasonable, during the time of Galileo, to believe that the earth was the center of the universe because that is what our senses told us was true, and certain scriptures seemed to support that.

This was Church doctrine at the time—as was the perfidy of the Jews, the rightness of slavery, the chattelism of women, and the evil of usury—and as fervently subscribed to then, as the denial of the priesthood to women is now.

Former president Jimmy Carter (2014) makes the discrimination against women case eloquently:

> There is a similar system of discrimination, extending far beyond a small geographical region to the entire globe; it touches every nation, perpetuating and expanding the trafficking in human slaves, body mutilation, and even legitimized murder on a massive scale. This system is based on the presumption that men and boys are superior to women and girls, and it is supported by some male religious leaders who distort the Holy Bible, the Koran, and other sacred texts to perpetuate their claim that females are, in some

27

basic ways, inferior to them, unqualified to serve God on equal terms. Many men disagree but remain quiet in order to enjoy the benefits of their dominant status. This false premise provides a justification for sexual discrimination in almost every realm of secular and religious life. (pp. 1-2)

Personal Aside #1

Being a man and writing about women in the Church is suspect and though I also have been marginalized due to my criminal/carceral status, my marginalization is self-inflicted, while women's is a fact of birth and historic teaching in the Church that women are the source of sin in the world.

The reason I never fully connected with the various religions I studied prior to becoming Catholic (Mormonism, New Age, Protestantism, and Judaism) is that, upon study—their theology, their morality, their praxis—broke down into contradiction and irrationality.

What attracted and held me within the Catholic Church was that the deeper I dug, the deeper I studied, the sounder, more beautiful, and more logical her theology, morality, and praxis became.

My path to the Catholic Church was an intellectual one; everything had to eventually align with reason, and this will be true within the ministries to the criminal/carceral world of the professional criminal: those who commit crimes for money and have made a conscious decision to live as a criminal based on the belief that the world is built upon criminality and one is either prey or predator.

As I begin this study I realize that, in many ways, this is the most significant study I've authored because it deals with the oldest oppression of human upon human, that of the man upon the woman.

St. Mary Magdalene

One of the cornerstones of the argument that only men can be priests comes from the documentation of the facts on the ground during Christ's ministry on earth, where the Church has consistently maintained that the leader of the apostles was Peter and it was upon him that the Church was built by Christ *and because* only men were chosen as apostles, only men can be ordained as priests.

Yet, Brock (2003) makes a good case that Mary Magdalene was the first apostle:

> Apostolic authority, without question, was a key issue in the early Christian churches. It insured that the one carrying the gospel message was a bona fide messenger. The criteria by which various early Christian authors attributed apostolic authority to certain followers of Jesus and not to others in early Christian documents provide insights into the politics of various factions of the early church. For example, Mary Magdalene was so esteemed among some early Christians that they bestowed on her the honorific title, "apostle to the apostles," and yet for others she holds no apostolic status at all and is instead known as a reformed prostitute, a concept for which there is no biblical basis.
> What did it take to be an apostle and were women included in that group? Hippolytus, an early

Christian bishop and martyr of Rome (ca. 170-ca. 236), wrote:

> Lest the female apostles doubt the angels, Christ himself came to them so that the women would be apostles of Christ and by their obedience rectify the sin of the ancient Eve....Christ showed himself to the (male) apostles and said to them..."It is I who appeared to these women and I who wanted to send them to you as apostles." (pp. 1-2)

If this is true, and I believe it is, because I cannot see how God approves the unequal status of women which the world has proclaimed since time immemorial.

And though it is generally agreed that the conflating of the three Marys is what led to the tradition that Mary Magdalene was a prostitute, theologians today separate them, as noted by Hinsdale (2011):

> Today all three major branches of Christianity (Roman Catholicism, Protestantism, and Orthodoxy) *do* distinguish between Mary Magdalene, Mary of Bethany and the sinner/penitent woman in Luke 7: 36-50. (p. 80)

I still believe the tradition of the Magdalene as a prostitute, as it resonates with me and more fully resonates with the scriptures as now canonized; and even the long attempt to separate her from prostitution seems an attempt to take away the power of penance in flowering the power of apostleship or Church leadership and the model of penance Christ conferred upon Magdalene seems unearned if she was merely a sinner, as all are, rather than a great sinner, a criminal sinner, a predatory sinner, a whore.

Many women theologians want her to have not been a prostitute as they see that as disempowering her, but Magdalene, having been a prostitute, or more accurately, according to Anne Catherine Emmerich (2005), a grand courtesan whose lovers were men of power and privilege who deeply captured by her exotic appearance and erotic potency; possessed dual powers from her sinful life which gave her, in her penitential life, apostolic authority:

> When the patrimony was divided, the castle of Magdalum fell by lot to Magdalen. It was a very beautiful building. Magdalen had often gone there with her family when she was a very young child, and she had always entertained a special preference for it. She was only about eleven years old when, with a large household of servants, men and maids, she retired thither and set up a splendid establishment for herself.
>
> Magdalum was a fortified place, consisting of several castles, public buildings and large squares of groves and gardens. It was eight hours east of Nazareth, about three from Capharnaum, one and a half from Bethsaida toward the south, and about a mile from the Lake of Genesareth. It was built on a slope of the mountain and extended down into the valley which stretches off toward the lake and around its shores. One of those castles belonged to Herod. He possessed a still larger one in the fertile region of Genesareth. Some of his soldiers were stationed in Magdalum, and they contributed there share to the general demoralization. The officers

31

were on intimate terms with Magdalen. There were, besides the troops, about two hundred people in Magdalum, chiefly officials, master builders, and servants.

The castle of Magdalum was the highest and most magnificent of all; from its roof one could see across the Sea of Galilee to the opposite shore. Five roads led to Magdalum, and on every one at one half-hours distance from the well-fortified place, stood a tower built over an arch. It was like a watchtower whence could be seen far into the distance. These towers had no connection with one another; they rose out of a country covered with gardens, fields, and meadows. Magdalen had men servants and maids, fields and herds, but a very disorderly household; all went to rack and ruin.
(pp. 3-4)

Mary Magdalene was the magnificently penitential woman who *was* the apostle to the apostles, called so by Christ, so clearly endorsed by his appearing to her first after his resurrection and by commissioning her to go tell the apostles that he had arisen; assuming the status of first among the apostles.

However, as Kienzle (1998) notes, quoting the Dominican Moneta of Cremona writing about the heretical Waldensians who allowed women preachers, this may not necessarily be a qualifier:

Christ sent Mary Magdalene to preach when he said in John 20:17: 'Go to my brethren and say to them: I am ascending to our Father and your Father, to my God and your God.' Mary Magdalene went and said to the disciples, 'I have seen the Lord.'" Moneta explains that the interpretation that Jesus sent her to preach should be ascribed to the distorted understanding of a heretic, because the Gospel author says only that she announced to the disciples, not that she preached. The Dominican author asks, "Now, whenever a woman is sent to announce something good to a church, should it be said that she preaches to that church?" His answer of course is "Non." (pp. 105-106)

St. Catherine of Siena

St. Catherine, one of two women Doctors of the Church, was a powerful mystic, member of the third order of the Dominicans, who only lived for 33 years (March 25, 1347 – April 29, 1380) but who, in her short life, exerted profound political influence during a time of turmoil in the Church where the popes reigned from Avignon, France; but she was able to influence Pope Gregory XI to return to Rome, cultivated by the revelations of St. Bridget of Sweden, as Gardner (1908) writes:

> Almost immediately after leaving the seclusion of her father's house, we find Catherine in touch with the politics of her native city, and with the great questions that were agitating the whole church. Not only are the spears and swords of contending factions lowered before her as she passes along the streets of Siena, but the princes and potentates of Italy seem to realize instantly that a new spiritual power has arisen in the land. From Avignon, the pope himself seemed to gladly know that there were secrets Christ had hidden from him, but not from the simple maiden.

This was due, in part, to the effect produced upon Pope Gregory XI's mind by the revelations of St. Bridget. From the beginning of his pontificate, the Swedish princess had exhorted him to repair the scandal caused by the defection of his predecessor. In a vision she heard the voice of the Blessed Virgin promising that if Gregory would restore the papal chair to Rome and reform the church, her prayers would flood his soul with spiritual joy from her divine Son. If not, the Blessed Virgin communicated to Bridget, Gregory would surely feel the rod of Christ's indignation, his life would be cut short, and he would be summoned to judgment. (pp. 63-64)

Ott (1909) notes, regarding St. Catherine's efforts with Pope Gregory XI:

Like the preceding popes of Avignon, Gregory XI made the fatal mistake of appointing Frenchmen, who did not understand the Italians and whom the Italians hated, as legates and governors of the ecclesiastical provinces in Italy. The Florentines, however, feared that a strengthening of the papal power in Italy would impair their own prestige in Central Italy and allied themselves with Bernabo in July, 1375. Both Bernabo and the Florentines did their utmost to stir up an insurrection in the pontifical territory among all those that were dissatisfied with the papal legates in Italy. They were so successful that within a short time the entire Patrimony of St. Peter was up in arms against the pope. Highly incensed at the seditious proceedings of the Florentines, Gregory XI imposed an extremely severe punishment upon them. He put Florence under interdict, excommunicated its inhabitants, and outlawed them and their possessions. The financial loss which the Florentines sustained thereby was inestimable. They sent St. Catherine of Siena to intercede for them with Gregory XI, but frustrated her efforts by continuing their hostilities against the pope. In the midst of these disturbances Gregory XI, yielding to the urgent prayers of St. Catherine, decided to remove the papal see to Rome, despite the protests of the French King and the majority of the cardinals. He left Avignon on 13 September, 1376, boarded the ship at Marsailles on 2 October, and came by way of Genoa to Corneto on 6 December. Here he remained until arrangements were made in Rome concerning its future government. On 13 January, 1377, he left Corneto, landed at Ostia on the following day, and sailed up the Tiber to the monastery of San Paolo, from where he solemnly made his entrance into Rome on 17 January. (n. p.)

In St. Catherine of Siena we have an example of a woman who was arguably more of a pope in spirit than Pope Gregory XI, who she essentially told to man up and get thee back to Rome from France; and he did.

As St. Catherine (2000) wrote in her first letter to Pope Gregory XI in Avignon:

> If till now you haven't been very firm in truth, I want you, I beg you, for the little time that is left, to be so—courageously and like a brave man—following Christ, whose vicar you are. And don't be afraid, father, no matter what may happen, of these blustery winds that have descended upon you—I

mean those rotten members who have rebelled against you. Don't be afraid, for divine help is near. Just attend to spiritual affairs, to appointing good pastors and administrators in your cities, for you have experienced rebellion because of bad pastors and administrators. Do something about it! And take heart in Christ Jesus and don't be afraid. Pursue and finish with true holy zeal what you have begun by holy intent—I mean your return [to Rome] and the sweet holy crusade. Delay no longer, for your delaying has already been the cause of a lot of trouble. The devil has done and is doing his best to keep this from happening, because he sees that he will be the loser.

Up, Father! No more irresponsibility! Raise the standard of the most holy cross, for it is with the fragrance of the cross that you will gain peace. I beg you to invite those who have rebelled against you to a holy peace, so that all this fighting can be diverted toward the unbelievers. I hope that God in his infinite goodness will send his help soon. Courage! Courage! Come, come to reassure God's poor servants, your children. They are waiting for you fondly, lovingly, longingly. (pp. 248-249)

Yes, St. Catherine of Siena is a Doctor of the Church and, as Gardiner (1908) notes, one of the most powerful and influential Catholic religious leaders during the chaotic 14th century:

During the summer of 1370 she received a series of special manifestations of Divine mysteries, which culminated in a prolonged trance, a kind of mystical death, in which she had a vision of Hell,

36

Purgatory, and Heaven, and heard a Divine command to leave her cell and enter the public life of the world. She began to dispatch letters to men and women in every condition of life, entered into correspondence with the princes and republics of Italy, was consulted by the papal legates about the affairs of the Church, and set herself to heal the wounds of her native land by staying the fury of civil war and the ravages of faction. She implored the pope, Gregory XI, to leave Avignon, to reform the clergy and the administration of the Papal States, and ardently threw herself into his design for a crusade, in the hopes of uniting the powers of Christendom against the infidels, and restoring peace to Italy by delivering her from the wandering companies of mercenary soldiers. (n. p.)

During the Middle Ages, religion was the only sector of society in which a woman, other than royalty, could exert a powerful influence on world affairs and Catherine was part of that, as Vecchio (1992) writes:

While the family played an increasingly important part in fifteenth-century culture and ideology, women, who had always been seen within the context of the family, increasingly were afforded little consideration. Religion was the only area in which, at least at a theoretical level, new ground was being broken for them. The debate over the existence of a female renaissance...has shown how women throughout the Middle Ages gradually lost out in terms of status, power, and "visibility."...one can talk about a female renaissance only in terms of the spiritual charisma accorded figures such as Catherine of Siena, Margery Kempe, Julian of

37

Norwich, and Catherine of Genoa is confirmed by fifteenth-century treatises on the family which reveal only one real novelty, that women had souls. (p. 135)

St. Catherine was a woman who was clearly able to be a priest, bishop, cardinal, or pope; and when a child, she dreamed of running away, putting on boys clothes and becoming a priest, noted by Undset (2009):

Catherine was for a time very much interested in the legend of St. Euphrosyne, who is supposed to have dressed as a boy and run away from home to enter a monastery. She toyed with the idea of doing the same herself.... (p. 10)

Kirsch (1909) writes about St. Euphrosyne:

Died about 470. Her story belongs to that group of legends which relate how Christian virgins, in order the more successfully to lead the life of celibacy and asceticism to which they had dedicated themselves, put on male attire and passed for men. According to the narrative of her life in the "Vitæ Patrum", Euphrosyne was the only daughter of Paphnutius, a rich man of Alexandria, who desired to marry her to a wealthy youth. But having consecrated her life to God and apparently seeing no other means of keeping this vow, she clothed herself as a man and under the name of Smaragdus gained admittance into a monastery of men near Alexandria, where she lived for thirty-eight years after. She soon attracted the attention of the abbot by the rapid strides which she made toward a perfect ascetic life, and when Paphnutius appealed to him for comfort in his sorrow, the abbot committed the latter to the care of the alleged young man Smaragdus. The father received from his own daughter, whom he failed to recognize, helpful advice and comforting exhortation. Not until she was dying did she reveal herself to him as his lost daughter Euphrosyne. After her death Paphnutius also entered the monastery. Her feast is celebrated in the Greek Church on 25 September, in the Roman Church on 16 January (by the Carmelites on 11 February). (n.p.)

Slavery

Women as chattels, as property of men and without virtually any rights at all, was accepted doctrine within the Church and throughout society until relatively a short time ago and is, even now, accepted religious dogma inscribed into law within much of the Islamic world.

In the Western world, women as co-equal with men has become the norm, and though still too often aligned with more in theory than practice, it has been intellectually established, solidly, that women can do virtually anything involved with being a priest as can men.

One of the central aspects of Catholic tradition which attracted me to the Church was its openness to anyone and walking the talk—acting on its words—especially around slavery and abortion, both of which the Church has condemned throughout its history, at least, as the orthodox histories I had read at that time, stated.

Further study uncovered the *Bull Romanus Pontifex* of Pope Nicholas V (1455, January 8), which changed my mind and left no doubt about papal support for slavery:

> ...since we had formerly by other letters of ours granted among other things free and ample faculty to the aforesaid King Alfonso -- to invade, search out, capture, vanquish, and subdue all Saracens and pagans whatsoever, and other enemies of Christ wheresoever placed, and the kingdoms, dukedoms, principalities, dominions, possessions, and all movable and immovable goods whatsoever held and possessed by them and to reduce their persons to perpetual slavery, and to apply and appropriate to himself and his successors the kingdoms, dukedoms, counties, principalities, dominions, possessions, and goods, and to convert them to his and their use and profit...

What is also consequential is that the *Bull* served as a foundation of many other conquests in the West, as Wikipedia notes:

> These passages specifically granted to nations and explorers the right to seek out lands unknown to Christians. In 1493 Pope Alexander VI issued the Bull *Inter Caetera* stating one Christian nation did not have the right to establish dominion over lands previously dominated by another Christian nation. Together, the *Dum Diversas*, the *Romanus Pontifex* and the *Inter Caetera* came to serve as a justification for the Discovery Doctrine and the Age of Imperialism. They were also early influences on the development of the slave trade of the 15th and 16th centuries, even though the papal bull *Sublimus*

Dei of 1537 forbade the enslavement of non-Christians. The executive brief for *Sublimus Dei* was withdrawn by the Pope after protests by the Spanish monarchy. Paul III publicly sanctioned slavery in Rome in 1545, the enslavement of Henry VIII in 1547 and the purchase of Muslim slaves in 1548.

Retrieved March 14, 2014 from http://en.wikipedia.org/wiki/Romanus_Pontifex

In the Church history which played a major role in my conversion, Crocker (2001) describes Pope Nicholas V, with no mention of this *Bull*:

Officially, the first of the Renaissance popes is Nicholas V (1147-1455)...He swept like a miracle through the courts of Germany and France, restoring papal prerogatives in Germany, getting the French to cooperate in offering the Council of Basel's antipope an honorable retirement, and amenably dissolving the Council itself. At the end of his reign he even achieved a peace concordat between nearly all the major city-states of Italy and the Kingdom of the Two Sicilies. As a Renaissance pope and a man of learning, he refounded the Vatican library with his own massive collection of books and began commissioning Italy's century of unparalleled architectural achievement. (pp. 212-213)

A few pages later, Crocker writes:

In 1537, for instance, at papal command, the Indians living in Spanish colonies were guaranteed

41

equal rights as fellow communicants in the Catholic Church. Under unstinting pressure from the Mexican bishop Bartolome de Las Casas—who had arrived in the New World with Columbus and was supported by Queen Isabella—the use of Indians as slaves was officially forbidden by Spanish law. (*Ibid.* p. 226)

But not apparently, by Catholic or Portuguese law.

The definitive word on slavery and the Church is from Noonan (2005):

> In 1993, in *Veritas splendor,* John Paul II saluted the *Catechism of the Catholic Church* as a "complete and full exposition of Christian moral teaching." In the same encyclical he used Vatican II's list of offenses against human dignity to illustrate the intrinsically evil, the acts incapable of being ordered to God. In the pope's presentation an offense to human dignity was intrinsic to the act of slaveholding. As already seen in chapter 1, the pope's teaching was that always and everywhere slavery is sinful.
>
> The old teaching of the Church on slavery taught that masters should allow their slaves the opportunity to practice religion and to marry and to perform the sexual duties of marriage. The Church taught that manumission was an act of charity so that being free was better than being slave. The offenses to human dignity that the Church did not condemn included the buying, selling hypothecating, inheriting, and owning of human beings; the use of slave labor without any measure

of just compensation; the denial to slaves of education, including instruction in reading and in writing, and the denial to slaves of the right to educate their children; the denial to slaves of any right to a religious vocation or to the sacrament of holy orders; the denial to slaves of the full range of conjugal companionship and protection; the denial of any right to personal development; and the complete exclusion of the slave from the political community. According to the teaching of John Paul II, all these denials and exclusions would be serious sins today. They were not denominated so by any magisterial document before the recent development of doctrine.

No special consciousness of the development in this matter was shown by the pope, who cited none of the old authorities approving the institution. Of moral theologians after St. Thomas, the pope mentioned only Ligouri, and then only peripherally. On the obligation to seek the truth he quoted Newman, "the distinguished defender of the rights of conscience," so Newman, the defender of development, was in his mind. John Paul himself spoke of the popes' efforts in the nineteenth and twentieth centuries to expound moral doctrine. "Fortified by the help of the Holy Spirit to a better comprehension of moral requirements in sexual matters and in familial, social, economic, and political matters, they have spoken. By their teaching, the continuous investigation of moral knowledge belongs to the tradition of the Church as it belongs to the history of the human race." Not in specific re-examination and reprobation of the old doctrine on slavery but in the broadest terms, the papal message endorsed the deepening of doctrine in morals. No better example was provided than the new teaching of the council, the new catechism, and the pope himself on slavery.

Neither the action of Vatican II, nor the teaching of the *Catechism,* nor the encyclical of the pope occasioned surprise or scandal among Catholics. The Church had always been against slavery. So thought that improbable stereotype, the average Catholic. No doubt most Catholics had been against slavery for a long time—at least since 1888 in Brazil and since 1865 in the United States and longer still in parts of Europe. In the recent formal condemnations the magisterium came into harmony with the thinking of the body of the faithful.

Only among persons with reason to be specifically concerned with the legacy of slavery was the change remarked. Notable among them were the Spiritans, the French missionary congregation that had labored in Africa and Cambodia. Their journal in 1999 published a special issue on the Church and slavery. As to the Church's past condemnations mentioned by Gregory XVI, an article asked, "What condemnation?" The issue as a whole bore the title *L'esclavage negation de l'humain*—Slavery, the negation of the human. Neither Leo XIII nor Gregory XVI, neither St. Thomas Aquinas nor St. Augustine, not even St. Paul himself would have dared to define the sin so powerfully and so exactly. (pp. 122-123)

We see in this the split of knowledge, between the average Catholic and between those who study or live the issues, and in the ministry to criminals, the ministry will have to come down on the side of those who study, for the criminals will study to see why they should forgo a narrative that matches their vision of the world enabling them to, in good conscience, be criminals.

Unfortunately, as with all human institutions, even this Catholic Church founded by God, confusion and contradiction will reign more often than not, though in the balance, the Church stands strong as walking the talk more than any other earthly institution throughout her more than 2,000 years of history.

Fr. Pierre Teilhard de Chardin

About a hundred years ago a French Jesuit, Fr. Pierre Teilhard de Chardin, began thinking and writing about a grand vision he had regarding Christ and Evolution; a vision so advanced that the Vatican theologians of the time could scarcely understand nor embrace it and forbade him from publishing his writing during his lifetime; he died in 1955.

Slowly however, after his death, as his work began to see the light of day, the Catholic theologians caught up and eventually even the popes realized how profound his work was and how much it would change the mind of the Church.

For a time, his actual faith was questioned through the complexity and speculative nature of his work, but as De Lubac (1967) makes clear, this concern was unnecessary:

Pere Teilhard's faith was as complete as it was ardent and firm. If he seemed to go beyond some positions generally adopted in the Church, he would never have been willing to lag behind any one of them. It was simply that it fell to him to explore truths which, without being new, stretched out like continents untrodden by man. "St. Paul and the Greek Fathers speak of a cosmic function of Christ: the exact content o that phrase has never been brought out." That was precisely what he would have liked to find in the theology of his time—more light on the 'organic and cosmic splendours contained in the Pauline doctrine of Chris gathering up all things.' The least, then, we can do is to recognize that he will have done more than any other man of our time to open up a vast field of inquiry for theologians, and that they must make it their business to apply themselves to it. (p. 203

That change is still in its infancy, but one root he helped plant, the clerical reevaluation of women from repository of sin and a dangerous being to be feared to a sister devoutly to be embraced, will someday lead to the creation of women priests, I am sure of it, I pray for it.

Chardin (1975) writes, in his brilliant essay on chastity, of embracing woman rather than fearing her; how true chastity lies on the other side of embrasure not at the foot of fear:

> By this I mean the idea—though 'impression' would be the better word—that sexual relations are tainted by some degradation or defilement. By the material conditions of its act; by the physical transports it

entails, by a sort of clouding of personality that accompanies it—'passion', man instinctively feels, has about it something of animality, of shame, of fever, of stupefaction, of fear, of mystery. Here we meet, in its most basic and most insistent form, and at its most acute, the *whole* intellectual and moral *problem of matter*. Sexuality is sinful. (p. 63)

And so it is with the chastity of the Church, true chastity lies on the other side of women becoming priests-bishops-cardinals-popes, beyond fearing them.

It is so clear that women have been acting functionally as priests in the Catholic Church in the past and should be now, that the circular arguments the institutional Church makes to justify not allowing women into the priesthood are an intellectual and moral embarrassment, virtually rendering Vatican pronouncements on any issue more suspect than they should be.

Evolution of matter and spirit—the work of humans co-creates future reality with God—marks a defining aspect of women in the Church, and where once it did signify virgin and mother, now, in an industrial and technological world reality co-created by God and humans, it no longer suffices; and as the Church ultimately accepted the sun's centrality in the solar system rather than the earths, it is past time to move away from the centrality of men to the Church, to a mutual and collaborative centrality of men and women, where each can become, priest, bishop, pope.

Ah, the evolution of all, of which human consciousness plays such an important role—imagine the human experience being synthesized from the super-rich in sixty million dollar penthouses in Hong Kong and Manhattan to busted-out homeless in Bowery corners and Brazilian favelas.

Every truth is His truth, the great convergence which draws all to Christ, as Fr. Teilhard taught us, and a truth still needing to be drawn to Christ's Vicar on earth is the truth of women's equality in all things, now and forever more; a great truth calling for women in the priesthood, women in the Curia, women on the papal throne; for as the Mother of God looks over us, and as Magdalene, Apostle to the Apostles and the closest companion of God on earth, has revealed to us, women are truly created in the image of God.

One of the reasons I feel combining women in the Church with Fr. Teilhard de Chardin is that he, of all the male Catholic theologians I have read, best explains the optimal relationship between the Church and women and as Chardin (1975) writes:

> *There is a general question of the feminine,* and so far it has been unsolved or imperfectly expressed by the Christian theory of sanctity. It is this that accounts for our dissatisfaction with, and our repugnance to, the old discipline of virtue. It used to be urged that the natural manifestations of love should be reduced as much as possible. We now see that the real problem is how to harness the energy they represent and transform them. We must not cut down on them, but go beyond them. Such will be our new ideal of chastity....
> This comparatively new proposition, that Christian perfection consists not so much in purifying oneself from the refuse of the earth as in divinizing creation, is a forward step. In the most conservative

quarters, it is beginning to be recognized that there is a communion with God through earth—a sacrament of the world—spreading like a halo around the Eucharist; but there is still a grudging reserve in allotting the share that has at last been accorded to terrestrial sources of nourishment. As in the biblical Eden, the majority of fruits are now allowed to the initiate. His, if he feels their attraction, the 'vocation'—his, the joys of artistic creation, the conquests of thought, the emotional excitement of discovery. These broadenings of personality are accepted as sanctifying or patient of sanctification. One tree, however, still carries the initial prohibition, the tree of the feminine. And so we are still faced by the same dilemma—either we can have woman only in marriage, or we must run away from the feminine. (Italics in original, pp. 71-74)

Chardin expands on the passion involved in this process, and its spiritual development:

Chastity attracts, and legitimately, by the aura of *freedom* which surrounds it. There are, it is true, tasks that call for the whole man; but on reflection it becomes apparent that the hindering or dividing agent is not Woman, but either the family or the physically loved woman. A noble passion lends wings. That is why the best test for determining to what degree a love is sublime would be to note to what degree it develops in the direction of a greater freedom of spirit. The more spiritual an affection is, the less it monopolizes—and the more it acts as a spur to action. (*Ibid. n.* 77)

49

The feminist movement in the West is over a hundred years old. Embracing the feminine as Teilhard envisioned within the Church is not yet realized, but today, October 18, 2013, as I write, there are rumors of women becoming cardinals, and even though the rumor was quickly shot down by the Vatican, those years could evaporate overnight in the illumination of the red hat on a woman's head.

These words from two doctors of the Church—one future, one present—are a cornerstone of evolution and faith upon which the future of Church praxis will be built; embracing the theology of Teilhard, who has understood and explained the Cosmic Christ, and Catherine who was—in practice—priest and pope during her fullest moments on earth.

Teilhard explains the evolution of matter, spirit and Catholic teaching; Catherine lived it.

We pray the Church will soon embrace her wisest daughters and sons.

Personal Aside #2

I am a Catholic convert baptized into the Church in 2004, am decidedly conservative, preferring the Latin Mass and the Church as seen by St. Thomas Aquinas, Pope John Paul II, Pope Benedict XVI, and Pope Francis; came into the Church after studying the works and attending meetings with Opus Dei; but have a life background that created many of my ideas in the 1960s American ferment.

All this being said, I find myself going against that Catholic tradition in the matter of women as priests and now fully believe they should be, for, as Cott (2013) wrote quoting Susan Sontag:

> ...I write partly in order to change myself so that once I write about something I don't have to think about it anymore. And when I write, it actually is to get rid of those ideas. (p. 123)

I have been following the Church pronouncements on this for some time but haven't really thought about it till now and as I read and think and write I am changing.

My heart tells me that women are equal to men in all things that priests do.

The Jesuits

Nowhere does the break between conservative and liberal Catholicism appear more disastrous than when reflecting upon this seminal issue of women in the Church.

Where the conservative popes proclaim women becoming priests an issue not even worth any more discussion, the Jesuits, in their 34th General Congregation, (Padberg, Ed. 2009) devoted special attention to women as equal partners in collaboration within Jesuit Ministry:

> **366/** 6. Church teaching certainly promotes the role of women within the family, but it also stresses the need for their contribution in the Church and in public life. It draws upon the text of Genesis which speaks of men and women created in the image of God (1:27) and the prophetic praxis of Jesus in his relationship with women. These sources call us to change our attitudes and work for a change of

structures. The original plan of God was for a loving relationship of respect, mutuality, and equality between men and women, and we are called to fulfill this plan. The tone of this ecclesial reflection on Scripture makes it clear that there is an urgency in the challenge to translate theory into practice not only outside but also within the Church itself.

The Role and Responsibility of Jesuits

367/ 7. The Society of Jesus accepts this challenge and our responsibility for doing what we can as men and as a male religious order. We do not pretend or claim to speak for women. However, we do speak out of what we have learned from women about ourselves and our relationship with them.

368/ 8 In making this response we are being faithful, in the changed consciousness of our times, to our mission; the service of faith, of which the promotion of justice is an absolute requirement. We respond, too, out of the acknowledgement of our own limited but significant influence as Jesuits and as male religious within the Church. We are conscious of the damage to the People of God brought about in some cultures by the alienation of women who no longer feel at home in the Church and who are not able with integrity to transmit Catholic values to their families, friends, and colleagues.

Conversion

369/ 9. In response, we Jesuits first ask God for the grace of conversion. We have been part of a civil and ecclesial tradition that has offended against women. And, like many men, we have a tendency to convince ourselves that there is not a problem. However unwittingly, we have often contributed to a form of clericalism which has reinforced male domination with an ostensibly divine sanction. By making this declaration we wish to react personally and collectively, and do what we can to change this regrettable situation. (pp. 616-617)

The Jesuit Pope Francis (2013) recently followed the lead of other popes in proclaiming his position regarding women as priests:

104. Demands that the legitimate rights of women be respected, based on the firm conviction that men and women are equal in dignity, present the Church with profound and challenging questions which cannot be lightly evaded. The reservation of the priesthood to males, as a sign of Christ the Spouse who gives himself in the Eucharist, is not a question open to discussion, but it can prove especially divisive if sacramental power is too closely identified with power in general. It must be remembered that when we speak of sacramental power "we are in the realm of function, not that of dignity or holiness". The ministerial priesthood is one means employed by Jesus for the service of his people, yet our great dignity derives from baptism, which is accessible to all. The configuration of the priest to Christ the head – namely, as the principal source of grace – does not imply an exaltation which would set him above others. In the Church, functions "do not favour the superiority of some vis-à-vis the others". Indeed, a woman, Mary, is more important than the bishops. Even when the function of ministerial priesthood is considered "hierarchical", it must be remembered that "it is totally ordered to the holiness of Christ's members". Its key and axis is not power understood as domination, but the power to administer the sacrament of the Eucharist; this is the origin of its authority, which is always a service to God's people. This presents a great challenge for pastors and theologians, who are in a position to recognize more fully what this entails with regard to the possible role of women in decision-making in different areas of the Church's life.

Pope Francis. (2013, November 24) *Apostolic Exhortation: Evangelii Gaudium* (#104)

And one wonders, how is something that is "not open to discussion" resonating within the world of women who are Catholics and women perhaps thinking of becoming Catholic?

As O'Neil (2014, February 24) puts it:

> That giant Achilles heel on the Catholic Church? Yeah, she's shaped like a woman. (n.p.)

There is no denying that the humble Pope Francis has changed some people's opinions of the Catholic Church for the better, but for many in the Western world, there's still the question of female equality in the Vatican. Namely, why can't women be priests, too, and how is it resonating within the minds of everyone who is Catholic and has thought through the issue—reading the pros and cons—on their own?

Chapter One

There are many convoluted theories accounting for woman's oppression throughout history and each of them that I have read have some element of truth to them; but regardless, it is obvious that women, virtually one half of the human family, have been—virtually across the global and historical board—treated as second-class citizens at best and as virtual slaves at worst; even too often, all too often, within first-class societies and including within the two major religions, Catholicism and Islam.

The silencing of women began a long time ago, as Beard (2014, February 14) notes:

> I want to start very near the beginning of the tradition of Western literature, and its first recorded example of a man telling a woman to 'shut up'; telling her that her voice was not to be heard in public. I'm thinking of a moment immortalised at the start of the Odyssey. We tend now to think of the Odyssey as the story of Odysseus and the adventures and scrapes he had returning home after the Trojan War – while for decades Penelope loyally waited for him, fending off the suitors who were pressing for her hand. But the Odyssey is just as much the story of Telemachus, the son of Odysseus and Penelope; the story of his growing up; how over the course of the poem he matures from boy to man. The process starts in the first book with Penelope coming down from her private quarters into the great hall, to find a bard performing to throngs of her suitors; he's singing

about the difficulties the Greek heroes are having in reaching home. She isn't amused, and in front of everyone she asks him to choose another, happier number. At which point young Telemachus intervenes: 'Mother,' he says, 'go back up into your quarters, and take up your own work, the loom and the distaff ... speech will be the business of men, all men, and of me most of all; for mine is the power in this household.' And off she goes, back upstairs.

There is something faintly ridiculous about this wet-behind-the-ears lad shutting up the savvy, middle-aged Penelope. But it's a nice demonstration that right where written evidence for Western culture starts, women's voices are not being heard in the public sphere; more than that, as Homer has it, an integral part of growing up, as a man, is learning to take control of public utterance and to silence the female of the species. The actual words Telemachus uses are significant too. When he says 'speech' is 'men's business', the word is muthos – not in the sense that it has come down to us of 'myth'. In Homeric Greek it signals authoritative public speech (not the kind of chatting, prattling or gossip that anyone – women included, or especially women – could do).

What interests me is the relationship between that classic Homeric moment of silencing a woman and some of the ways women's voices are not publicly heard in our own contemporary culture, and in our own politics from the front bench to the shop floor. It's a well-known deafness that's nicely parodied in the old Punch cartoon: 'That's an excellent suggestion, Miss Triggs. Perhaps one of the men here would like to make it.' I want to look too at how it might relate to the abuse that many women who do speak out are subjected to even now, and one of the questions at the back of my mind is the connection between publicly speaking out in support of a female logo on a banknote, Twitter threats of rape and decapitation, and Telemachus' put-down of Penelope. (n.p.)

Retrieved   March   10,   2014   from http://www.lrb.co.uk/2014/02/14/mary-beard/the-public-voice-of-women

Personal Aside #3

I had largely forgotten the women's movement, what I had learned about it and believed during the Sixties—other than noting the horrors of the oppression of women internationally within the third world; as the status of women in America seemed approaching parity on a steady upward trajectory—it was generally assumed we would soon have a women president.

It is now obvious to me that it is time—it is past time—that the Catholic Church once again open the process of study, prayer and reflection that will surely lead to a dramatic increase of women in Catholic leadership at the highest levels, including ordination as priests.

This is what should have happened—much evidence says did happen—from the beginning days of the Church, and one can only dream of the difference this would have made in the world where the most organized institution in the Western world gave full equality to women; and how would this have impacted the deep historical subjugation of women that even now inflicts too much of the Eastern world.

I reached this conclusion after several months of study and as I continued my studies of women religious in the Church, the time came to begin examining the opposing views as I have always found it imperative to research the thought leaders on each side of an argument important to me. Since I have already been doing so on the hierarchical Church position for some time—at least in terms of general Church teaching—I ventured to do so on the position of the women religious and accessed several crucial works about the issue.

Women's Ordination Conference

One of the most important organizing events for women's ordination was the Women's Ordination Conference of 1975 in Detroit, where Rosemary Radford Ruether (1976) writes:

> Patriarchy not only pervades specific dictates about women, but also creates an entire symbolic edifice of reality that reflects the social hierarchy of male dominance and female submission. The symbolism of God as a patriarchal male, and nature as passively female; the portraying of the Messiah as a warrior, king and judge, lord over a passive, female Church; the same symbolism of minister as ruling male over a passive, feminized, infantilized laity, is simply the projection on the level of theology, ecclesiology and ministry of this same patriarchal hierarchy of male over female. The challenge of male dominance, therefore, challenges the entire symbolic language of order, hierarchy, power,

lordship and authority in religion, as these have been shaped by patriarchy.

Can structures so deep-rooted be changed? The answer we must give is that they must be, for the sake of the Gospel itself. The Gospel, rooted in the unitary personhood of all humans, in the image of God, restored in Christ, is about the liberation of humanity from all orders of oppression and idolatry. Male dominance must be recognized as simply one of those systems of injustice that is to be overcome by the Gospel. Dressed up in the language of God, Christ and the Church, male dominance becomes idolatry, the projection of the vanities of human egoism and unjust power upon the very face of God. For that reason it is truly anathema, and all Christians, male and female, must come to look upon it with the horror and disgust it deserves, rather than continuing to cower before its presumptive authority. (p. 31)

Well said, well said, yet we still have a ways to go within the Catholic Church before this it truly becomes 'anathema'.

At the same conference Elizabeth Schussler Fiorenza (1976) provides a cogent, succinct response to one of the key arguments denying women the priesthood: that it is biblically based on Christ and his Apostles' ministry in Palestine:

The theological self-understanding of this early Christian movement is best expressed in the baptismal formula Galatians 3:27-29. In reciting this formula the newly initiated Christians

59

proclaimed their vision of an inclusive community. Over and against the cultural-religious pattern shared by Hellenists and Jews alike, the Christians affirmed that all social, political and religious differences were abolished in Jesus Christ. The self-understanding of the Christian community eliminated all distinctions of religion, race, class and caste, and thereby allowed not only gentiles and slaves to assume full leadership in the Christian community, but also women. Women were not marginal figures in this movement, but exercised leadership as apostles, prophets, evangelists, missionaries, offices similar to that of Barnabas, Apollos or Paul.

The controversies of Paul with his opponents prove that the leadership of *apostles* was most significant for the nascent Christian movement. According to Paul, apostleship is not limited to the twelve. All those Christians are apostles who were eyewitnesses to the resurrection and who were commissioned by the resurrected Lord to missionary work (I Corinthians 9:4). According to Luke only those Christians were eligible to replace Judas who accompanied Jesus in his Galilean ministry and were also eyewitnesses to his resurrection (Acts 1:21). According to all four Gospels women fulfilled these criteria of apostleship enumerated by Paul and Luke. Women accompanied Jesus from Galilee to Jerusalem and witnessed his death (Mark 14:40). Moreover, women were according to all criteria of historical authenticity the first witnesses of the resurrection, for this fact could not have been derived from Judaism nor invented by the primitive Church.

That these women were not left anonymous but identified by name suggests that they played an important role in the Christian movement in Palestine. Their leader appears to have been Mary Magdalene since all four Gospels transmit her name, whereas the names of the other women vary. Thus, according to the Gospel traditions women were the primary apostolic witnesses for the fundamental data of the early Christian faith: they were eyewitnesses of Jesus's ministry, his death, his burial and his resurrection. (95-96)

This benchmark established by Paul and Luke, is an argument that it is difficult to see how it has been ignored for these two thousand years; except through the machinations of the universal belief in female inferiority.

Personal Aside #4

As I began reading the Catholic feminist material I realized again, that of all the liberation movements, that of women was the mother of them all; and as I read about the seminal liberation movement in relation to the Catholic Church, from the perspective of women religious, I realized how right they are, more, how right both positions are.

Women have been oppressed within the Church since Genesis and they are right to struggle against it, and the Church is right to struggle to protect Church tradition, but the Church must ultimately bow to reason, the benchmark of truth.

Two seminal women of the West whose secular writing captured my attention in this regard were Mary Parker Follett and Simone de Beauvoir, with de Beauvoir's magisterial work, *The Second Sex*, which must be read in its unabridged edition, translated by Constance Borde and Sheila Malovany-Chevallier, published by Alfred A, Knopf (2012).

More about Follett later.

Fr. Teilhard & Joseph Campbell

The connection Teilhard de Chardin made between Catholicism and evolution is obvious almost a century later; that spirit and matter evolve, that they converge, that we are our body and soul.

Free will is the determinative factor. Free will explains the oft appearing herky jerky movement that is actually ascension, and it is so with the women in the Church, who will someday, as Dr. Clarissa Pinkola Estes so eloquently puts it in the title of her book: *Untie the Strong Woman.*

We are part of the convergence of Joseph Campbell's mythicness and Teilhard's mysticism.

We see a convergence of the Wise Woman and the Holy Father and when we see that convergence, our children will rejoice.

Campbell (1988) notes the importance of myth:

> Greek and Latin and biblical literature used to be part of everyone's education. Now, when these were dropped, a whole tradition of Occidental mythological information was lost. It used to be that these stories were in the minds of people. When the story is in your mind, then you see its

62

relevance to something happening in your own life. It gives you perspective on what's happening to you. With the loss of that, we've really lost something because we don't have a comparable literature to take its place. These bits of information from ancient times, which have to do with the themes that have supported human life, built civilizations, and informed religions over the millennia, have to do with deep inner problems, inner mysteries, inner thresholds of passage, and if you don't know what the guide-signs are along the way, you have to work it out yourself. (p. 4)

What Campbell called myth, is, for us, religious truth, the highest truth; but in his search for meaning and the journey to truth, he sparked deep conversations among non-religious about the truth of myth, for in the great stories from the mythical traditions of the world lay clear truths, universal truths, that have been gathered and embroidered into a wondrous tapestry under the rubrics Christ gave us.

Boff (1987) comments on the power of myth:

History simply recounts. It really tells us almost nothing. Theology understands. It is conceptual, and this is better. But we want more. Life calls for realization, life postulates depth. Life will have celebration and exaltation. But in order to celebrate, it is not enough just to hear a formula. It is not enough even to know and reflect. We must open our heart, we must project our enthusiasm outward. We must magnify what we wish to celebrate. Praise and enthusiasm thrive in grandiloquence, exaltation, excess. Generosity and exuberance are of the essence of festival. Here is where image, symbol, myth, and archetype appear. None of this, however, is invention of reality, but only its exaltation and sublimation. In history and theology, reason speaks: *logos*. Symbol expresses the heart: *pathos*. It is merely a matter of two different approaches to the same reality. History tells; reason seeks explanations; and symbol uncovers meaning. (p. 207)

Before Christ, the Jews were the Church and after Christ the Catholics were the Church; yet both are and will forever remain, the People of God.

An article in *America Magazine* from the leader of The National Leadership Roundtable on Church Management about meetings in 2013 with Curial leadership in Rome makes a good case:

My colleagues and I learned a long time ago that to do nothing is to be complicit, so we welcomed the opportunity to go to Rome to promote the role of women. Our passion for this goal comes, in part, from the belief that women deserve to be equally valued, to experience being equally valued and to be entrusted with leadership and decision-making responsibilities in the church. The dignity of the human person, equally accorded, is at the heart of Christianity. Yet our passion for these conversations is also deeply rooted in our conviction that valued female leadership is what the church deserves and needs in order to grow in its potential and to be more effective in its mission. By failing to attend properly to the leadership of women, the church misses out on the talent of half of the people made in the image and likeness of God to further its mission. Women bring unique experiences and alternative approaches to challenges. When companies and governments augment the percentage of women in leadership, prosperity increases. The church would likewise benefit, in terms of spiritual riches....

During our visits practical solutions are proffered in earnest and discussed in detail: Expand the number of women in professional roles in each dicastery. Increase the number of women who serve on advisory councils to each pontifical congregation and council, and expand the pool of candidates who are called to serve in such advisory roles. Restore women to diaconal ministry. Appoint women to the diplomatic corps and to the communications apostolate. Ensure in the selection of bishops that criteria include a candidate's ability to relate well to women. Review the current Lectionary and reclaim the many Scriptural passages with women as protagonists that have been left out of the readings heard at Mass. Ponder the effect and impact such exclusion has had over time in the catechesis and participation of women and girls in the life of the church....

Our discussions and recommendations include the aspirational and practical. We offer simple, immediate steps that can be taken and more detailed projects requiring hard work and perseverance. A practical proposal we have championed is providing day care at the Vatican so that parents and especially mothers of young children who work there have safe, reliable and convenient child care. Likewise we have recommended that a network of women working in the Vatican be formed to support and promote one another.

We recognize that there are far more ideas worthy of consideration and action, and we encourage a global discussion among the faithful. What are the obstacles that might be removed in order to appoint lay women to the College of Cardinals? Perhaps Pope Francis could invite women to join his committee of advisors on reforming the Curia. Perhaps he could establish a Council for the Promotion of Women in the Church, and recruit women (and men) from every continent to serve.

The church should make use of the expertise of women religious who have served in congregational leadership at the international level. Must leadership in each and every instance require ordination? For symbolic reasons alone these appointments would be stunning, but also the decisions would reflect how much the church stands to benefit from such perspective and expertise. Strategies for evangelization would be significantly strengthened by the input of women. Women can help our beloved church be holier, more effective, more relevant, more welcoming and more faithful in its mission. (n.p.)

Retrieved October 19, 2013 from http://americamagazine.org/issue/opening-doors

Personal Aside #5

What is becoming clear to me after all the research is that the patterns of thought and action within the Leadership Conference of Women Religious (LCWR) reflects decades of practice within many of the communities of women religious that is based on a feminism that is itself based on years of feminist scholar's research that leads to conclusions which will probably not be changed at a personal level, conclusions which are deeply embedded.

In every paradigm change I have experienced, there has often been an intellectual hinge, an idea that answers the chaos of the past, creating a future unity.

In my conversion to Catholicism it was the scripture Matthew 16:18: "Thou art Peter; and upon this rock I will build my church, and the gates of hell shall not prevail against it."

In my coming to believe in the rightness of women priests, it was the response to: "Christ only selected men as apostles", yes, but he also only selected Jews.

Papal Perspectives

The discussion around women's ordination has been intense, but, in this year of the 20th annual anniversary of one of the seminal papal documents, the Apostolic Letter, *Ordinatio Sacerdotalis*, On Reserving Priestly Ordination to Men Alone, by Pope John Paul II (1994), let us look at the opening paragraph in which the Holy Father wrote:

> When the question of the ordination of women arose in the Anglican Communion, Pope Paul VI,

out of fidelity to his office of safeguarding the Apostolic Tradition, and also with a view to removing a new obstacle placed in the way of Christian unity, reminded Anglicans of the position of the Catholic Church: "She holds that it is not admissible to ordain women to the priesthood, for very fundamental reasons. These reasons include: the example recorded in the Sacred Scriptures of Christ choosing his Apostles only from among men; the constant practice of the Church, which has imitated Christ in choosing only men; and her living teaching authority which has consistently held that the exclusion of women from the priesthood is in accordance with God's plan for his Church." (Paragraph 1)

Retrieved February 23, 2014 from
http://www.vatican.va/holy_father/john_paul_ii/apost_l
etters/1994/documents/hf_jp-
ii_apl_19940522_ordinatio-sacerdotalis_en.html

With all due respect to John Paul II whose writings and papacy played a major role in my conversion, the reason exhibited here is very weak: that Christ only chose men and the Church has maintained that tradition and the consistency of that teaching authority.

This is actually only one reason, Christ chose only men, with the other two merely praxis of the first.

Yes, Christ only selected men to be apostles; and the response from women religious, yes, but he also only selected Jews, and no one is saying that only Jews can become priests.

Sometimes the most elaborate edifice falls from the weakness of one rock; and sometimes an eternal cathedral is built upon the strength of one rock.

Patriarchy in the Catholic Church is so accepted that Pope Francis recently accused Eve of dialoguing with the devil rather than choosing to follow the word of God, but, when we read the Bible about this episode:

> 1] Now the serpent was more subtle than any other wild creature that the LORD God had made. He said to the woman, "Did God say, 'You shall not eat of any tree of the garden'?" 2] And the woman said to the serpent, "We may eat of the fruit of the trees of the garden; 3] but God said, 'You shall not eat of the fruit of the tree which is in the midst of the garden, neither shall you touch it, lest you die.'"
> 4] But the serpent said to the woman, "You will not die. 5] For God knows that when you eat of it your eyes will be opened, and you will be like God, knowing good and evil." (Genesis 3:1-5)

We see that Eve did not dialogue with the devil but repeated the instruction the Lord gave her; but Satan lied to her and told her she would not die, and she believed him, which caused her moment of weakness, leading to the Original Sin, humans acting from their free will.

As noted in the Vatican Information Service (2014, March 10):

> Vatican City, 10 March 2014 (VIS) – At midday today, the first Sunday of Lent, the Holy Father appeared at the window of his study to pray the Angelus with the faithful gathered in St. Peter's

Square. The Bishop of Rome commented that every year the Gospel of the first Sunday of Lent presents Jesus' temptations, and he mentioned that the tempter seeks to divert the Lord from His Father's plan, or rather the way of sacrifice that involves offering Himself in atonement and with love, and attempts to make Him choose the easy path of success and power.

"Indeed, the devil, to divert Jesus from the way of the cross, presents Him with false messianic hopes: economic well-being, as indicated by the possibility of turning stones into bread; a miraculous and spectacular style as seen in the idea of throwing Himself off the highest point of the temple of Jerusalem, to be saved by angels, and finally a shortcut to power and domination, in exchange for His open worship of Satan".

Jesus, the Pope explained, "firmly rejects all these temptations and reiterates His determination to follow the path set out by the Father, without compromising with sin and with the logic of the world. ... This is why Jesus, instead of entering into a dialogue like Eve, chooses to take refuge in God's Word and responds with the power of this Word. We should remember this when we are tempted ourselves: do not argue with Satan, always defend ourselves with the Word of God. And this will save us". (n.p.)

The concept that Eve—women—are weak and more subject to sin than men is so normative within the Church, even simple daily comments reinforce it, incorrectly as in this case.

Chapter Two

Spiritual Evolution

Some of the foundational ideas of the women religious seem to be connected to the work of Teilhard de Chardin S. J. (work which stresses the evolutionary nature of matter and spirit) and with his ideas being more accepted by the Church in recent years—he was prohibited from publishing while he was alive—it gives some concreteness, especially in the minds of women religious, to their own ideas.

While examining the ideas and strategies of the dissenting women religious—and we use the word dissenting advisedly as there can be found scriptural validation of their position, especially in Galatians 3:28: "There is neither Jew nor Greek, there is neither slave nor free person; there is not male and female; for you are all one in Christ Jesus."—we definitely have to take into account the absolutely vile history of humankind in its treatment of women, still being practiced in all too many countries; and in the development of feminist theology within the Catholic Church and without, we have to give it the same level of personhood's determinative final value (very little) as we do to the corrupted social/familial structures within which many criminals grew up, blaming that on why they became criminals.

That structural brutality and oppression of women was, and is, still true, is horrific and tragic; but once adulthood is reached and it becomes time to put away childish things, even the bad ones, we all, through dedicated prayer and studying of the essential earthly goodness and divine birth of our Church, can learn that our true human nature is to know and love God and that knowing and that loving is most completely discovered through the sacramental life of the Roman Catholic Church.

Everything sound the Church teaches stands on reason which even the laity understand, but when they no longer understand, it is no longer believed, and for decades now, many Catholics have accepted women as having the standing to become priests; and had women been priests, there would very possibly not have been a world-wide scandal of sexually abused children.

This issue is one sapping the passion of the Church; the unwillingness to acknowledge the reasonableness and rightness of women priests as the kind of change that will rekindle the eternal fire of the pilgrim Church and restrengthen the barque of Peter.

Mea culpas are demanded, yes, but penance is healthy, as healthy for the Church as for its members.

As the Holy Father has sought forgiveness from the Jews so should he seek if from women and it will be given in a mighty wave washing though Holy Mother Church with Pentecostal power.

More Papal Perspectives

The mantra of the three popes, John Paul, Benedict and Francis, has been that the issue is one not even open to discussion anymore; though from *Women in Canon Law* in 1975 by the Canon Law Society of America, through *Decree on the Attempted Priestly Ordination of Some*

Catholic Women in 2002 by the Congregation for the Doctrine of the Faith, and the 26 other documents from either the Vatican, the U.S. Bishop's Conference, Catholic Orders like the Jesuits, or Catholic Theological Societies, it has been discussed continuously; summaries of which are included in the magisterial book by Halter (2004), *The Papal No: A Comprehensive Guide to the Vatican's Rejection of Women's Ordination.*

One gets the distinct impression that what the popes are really saying is that they *do not wish* to discuss this issue any longer, as the longer it is discussed the more feeble the reasoning for denying women the priesthood becomes:

- Christ called only men, but he also called only Jews
- Christ incarnated as a man, but how else would he incarnate as in first century Israel women barely existed in any legal sense and surely even less in a religious sense.
- Women are inferior, an idiocy made even more idiotic in the 20th century and beyond.
- Christ as groom of the Church as bride, a theological argument hardly relevant, ever, in the context that Christ is Almighty God, creator of all things, neither man nor woman, both man and woman.
- It is tradition, but supporting slavery was also a Church tradition for millennia, but as social conditions changed, it changed.

Boff (1987) puts the attempt to stop questioning in proper perspective:

73

Pride and unbridled ambition are not in the quantity of questioning, but in the establishment of preposterous answers. There are no limits on asking. The faculty of inquiry is inhabited by a wild "demon"—the divine in us. Despotism always begins by prohibiting any questions. To forbid questions is to deprive the truth of its right to manifest itself. One who never asks questions is deprived of the warming, beneficent light of the encounter with supreme Truth. (p. 21)

Sexual Abuse in the Church

We have to wonder how much the news of the purported homosexual lobby within the Vatican plays in the lack of willingness to continue the discussion of women as priests.

Recent news from *Catholic World News* (2014, January 20) reported:

> A former commandant of the Swiss Guard has confirmed the existence of an influential "gay lobby" within the Vatican.

> "I know from personal experience that the gay lobby exists," Elmar Mäder, who was head of the Swiss Guard from 2002 to 2008, told the Swiss weekly Schweiz am Sonntag. He was questioned about reports earlier this month, in which an unidentified member of the Swiss Guard had claimed that he had been the target of sexual advances made by a number of officials of the Roman Curia.

Mäder said that active homosexuals within the Vatican comprise a virtual "secret society." He added that because they are more loyal to each other than to the Holy See, "it becomes a security risk." (n.p.)

To obtain more depth on this subject, accessing two magisterial works on it: *The Rite of Sodomy: Homosexuality and the Roman Catholic Church* by Randy Engel, and *Sacrilege: Sexual Abuse in the Catholic Church* by Leon J. Podles, both devout Catholics, provides that.

Reading these books is a horrifying walk in the sewer—especially painful for Catholics—but a vital walk to understand what has happened in the Church, not only in the present, but for centuries, which Engels book covers, while Podles book focuses on the modern scandal in the United States.

Mary Parker Follett

Isn't the noosphere—the concept Teilhard de Chardin learned from Russian scientist Vladimir Ivanovich Vernadsky and Christianized—the global vision of Mary Parker Follett's dream of group evolution, where every blogger, internet commenter and twitter tweeter contributes to the electronic internet group shaping our new reality.

One of the characteristics of the current struggle between the women religious of the Leadership Conference of Women Religious (LCWR) and the Vatican, is that it is a classic case of group negotiating as studied by Mary Parker Follett who felt human definitions, human's highest selfhood, came from working within a group, not alone as individuals.

Both groups—the LCWR and the Vatican—operate from a group formed psychology, but only that of the women moves and grows as Follett had hoped, while the Vatican, the papacy and attendant cardinals/bishops move in lockstep according to a matrix established—as it claims—at the beginnings of the Church, yet words, ideas and events also established at the beginnings of the Church counteract the locksteps, taking the ground from beneath their feet, the most powerful being:

> **26]** For you are all the children of God by faith, in Christ Jesus. **[27]** For as many of you as have been baptized in Christ, have put on Christ. **[28]** There is neither Jew nor Greek: there is neither bond nor free: there is neither male nor female. For you are all one in Christ Jesus. **[29]** And if you be Christ's, then are you the seed of Abraham, heirs according to the promise. (Galatians 3:26-29)

The saddest result of Follett's exclusion from the canon of management thinkers during her life and after was the loss of her vision added to the body of work—virtually all by men—taught in the academy.

What she specialized in was retaining the emotional content of individual lives in the rather dry and objectified writings of male management theorists; but it was not to be until decades later, when men—most of who were influenced by her writings—began introducing the personal perspective.

Follett (1951) also pioneered the concept of power-with rather than power-over, which she notes:

> Genuine power can only be grown, it will slip from every arbitrary hand that grasps it; for genuine power is not coercive control, but coactive control. Coercive power is the source of the universe; coactive power, the enrichment and advancement of every human soul. (p. xiii)

This is the model of the archetypical loss of women's collaborative leadership the Catholic Church has been suffering from for 2,000 years, but over the past few decades' Catholic feminist theologians have been changing it, as Henold (2008) writes:

> Battered by patriarchy and the daily indignities of sexism in the church, Catholic feminists not only outlined a new vision for the church, they also claimed that this vision was legitimately Catholic by defining it as such. As "the church" they had a right to do so if they followed the precepts of justice. This is not "cafeteria-style" Catholicism, where Catholics pick and choose what they want to believe. This is a liberated Catholicism in which Catholic women understand that the unjust institutional power structure does not have the power to define them, or imprison them, or even reject them. Its ability to have "power over" has greatly diminished. In this view, the people of God have a right and an obligation to define what it means to be Catholic in the world, and Catholic feminists were, and remain, some of the most visible and strongest advocates of that view. (p. 243)

With Margaret Thatcher, also from a humble background but who also rose, like Golda Meir, to become a globally recognized leader and important shaper of global history, we see the fallacy, the idiocy, of refusing to discuss the question of women as leaders in the Catholic Church, for it is only from the ranks of the priesthood that Catholic leadership arises and women are banned from the priesthood.

Golda Meir (1975) writes about her experience when asked by Ben-Gurion to become the Minister of Labor in the first cabinet of the new state of Israel:

> The religious bloc balked a bit at the idea of a woman minister but eventually accepted the argument that in ancient Israel Deborah had been a judge—which was at least equivalent to, if not more important than being, a cabinet minister! (p. 255)

Ms. Meir wrote about her service:

> My seven years in the Ministry of Labor were, without doubt, the most satisfying and the happiest of my life. (*Ibid.* p. 256)

This Old Testament argument with Deborah as foil still has teeth, as noted by Wikipedia:

> Deborah...was a prophetess of the God of the Israelites, the fourth Judge of pre-monarchic Israel, counselor, warrior, and the wife of Lapidoth according to the Book of Judges chapters 4 and 5. The only female judge mentioned in the Bible, Deborah led a successful counterattack against the forces of Jabin king of Canaan and his military

78

commander Sisera, the narrative is recounted in chapter 4.

Judges chapter 5 gives the same story in poetic form. This passage, often called The Song of Deborah, may date to as early as the 12th century BC and is perhaps the earliest sample of Hebrew poetry. It is also significant because it is one of the oldest passages that portrays fighting women, the account being that of Jael, the wife of Heber, a Kenite tent maker. Jael killed Sisera by driving a tent peg through his temple as he slept. Both Deborah and Jael are portrayed as strong independent women. The poem may have been included in the Book of the Wars of the Lord mentioned in Numbers 21:14.

In the Book of Judges, it is stated that Deborah was a judge of Israel and the wife of Lapidoth, (the name means "torches"). (Judges 4:4) She rendered her judgments beneath a palm tree between Ramah in Benjamin and Bethel in the land of Ephraim. (Judges 4:5) Some people today refer to Deborah as the mother of Israel, as she is titled in the Biblical "Song of Deborah and Barak" (Judges 5:7).

Retrieved March 17, 2014 from http://en.wikipedia.org/wiki/Deborah

Fr. Teilhard

In my opinion, because of the depth and breadth of Fr. Teilhard's theological speculations, it will be some time before the Church properly understands him and gives him his earned position in her universe of Doctors of the

Church; but as much as St. Thomas Aquinas' thought determined the medieval Church, and guides her still; Fr. Teilhard's thought will shape and guide her in the future; but it could be a century or so before he is finally and deeply appreciated.

In a quote attributed to Fr. Thomas Berry, a former president of the American Teilhard Association who also felt Fr. Teilhard de Chardin's importance will grow, as noted in the introduction to the new translation of Chardin's *The Phenomena of Man*, entitled *The Human Phenomena* (2003):

> "To see as Teilhard saw is a challenge, but increasingly his vision is becoming available to us. I fully expect that in the next millennium Teilhard will be generally regarded as the fourth major thinker of the western Christian tradition. These would be St. Paul, Augustine, Thomas Aquinas, and Teilhard." (p. xiv)

Pope Emeritus Benedict (2004) understood Teilhard's immense value to Catholic theological thinking today, commenting on Johannine theology about Christ drawing all things to himself: [30] Jesus answered, and said: This voice came not because of me, but for your sakes. [31] Now is the judgment of the world: now shall the prince of this world be cast out. [32] And I, if I be lifted up from the earth, will draw all things to myself. (John 12:30-32):

> It must be regarded as an important service of Teilhard de Chardin's that he rethought these ideas from the angle of the modern view of the world and, in spite of a not entirely unobjectionable tendency toward the biological approach, nevertheless on the

whole grasped them correctly and in any case made them accessible once again. (p. 236)

In another work, Pope Emeritus Benedict (2000) wrote:

In a sense, creation is history.

This can be understood in several ways. For example, against the background of the modern evolutionary world view, Teilhard de Chardin depicted the cosmos as a process of ascent, a series of unions. From very simple beginnings the path leads to ever greater and more complex unities, in which multiplicity is not abolished but merged into a growing synthesis, leading to the "Noosphere", in which spirit and its understanding embrace the whole and are blended into a kind of living organism. Invoking the epistles to the Ephesians and Colossians, Teilhard looks on Christ as the energy that strives toward the Noosphere and finally incorporates everything in its "fullness'. From here Teilhard went on to give a new meaning to Christian worship: the transubstantiated Host is the anticipation of the transformation and divinization of matter in the Christological "fullness". In his view, the Eucharist provides the movement of the cosmos with its direction; it anticipates its goal and at the same time urges it on. (pp.28-29)

Fr. Pierre Teilhard de Chardin, S.J. was one of the most extraordinary Catholic thinkers of the modern age; but, he was also a man of action as indicated by the list of citations from his war service as a medical orderly in World War I, noted in Chardin, *Making of a Mind*, (1965):

Pierre Teilhard de Chardin, registered for non-combatant duties in 1902 and again in 1904, had never done his military service. In December 1914 a recruiting board passed him as 'fit for active service'. He was called up almost immediately and posted as a medical orderly to the 13th infantry section of a unit stationed first at Vichy and later at Clermont-Ferrand. He left for the front on 20th January 1915, as a stretcher-bearer, 2nd class, in the 8th regiment of Moroccan light infantry (Tirailleurs), which on 23rd June 1915 became the 4th mixed regiment of Zouaves and Moroccan Tirailleurs. On 13th May 1915 he was promoted to corporal.

Citations

29th August 1915. *Cited in Divisional Orders.* 'Volunteered to leave the aid-post in order to serve in the front-line trenches. Displayed the greatest self-sacrifice and contempt for danger.'

17th September 1916. *Cited in Army Orders.* 'A model of bravery, self-sacrifice, and coolness. From the 15th to the 19th August he directed the teams of stretcher-bearers over ground torn by shell-fire and swept by machine guns. On the 18th August he went out to within 20 yards of the enemy lines to retrieve the body of a fallen officer and brought it back to the trenches.'

20th June 1917. *Medaille Militaire.* 'A first-rate N.C.O. His sterling character has won him confidence and respect. On 20th May 1917 he deliberately entered a trench under heavy bombardment to bring back a casualty.'

21ˢᵗ May 1921. *At the request of his old regiment he was made Chevalier of the Legion d' Honneur.* 'An outstanding stretcher-bearer, who during four years of active service, was in every battle and engagement the regiment took part in, applying to remain in the ranks in order that he might be with the men, whose dangers and hardships he constantly shared.' (p. 41)

Wikipedia describes the *Médaille militaire*:

The Médaille militaire (English: Military Medal) is a military decoration of the French Republic first established in 1852 by Emperor Napoleon III for award to privates and non-commissioned officers who distinguished themselves by acts of bravery in action against an enemy force. He may have taken his inspiration from a medal established and awarded by his father, Louis Bonaparte, King of Holland. An interesting feature of the médaille is that it is also the supreme award for leadership, being awarded to generals and admirals who had been commanders-in-chief. This particular médaille is considered superior even to the grand cross of the Légion d'honneur.

(Retrieved November 28, 2013 from http://en.wikipedia.org/wiki/M%C3%A9daille_militaire)

And the *Legion d'honneur*:

The Legion of Honour, or in full the National Order of the Legion of Honour (French: Ordre national de la Légion d'honneur) is a French order established by Napoleon Bonaparte on 19 May 1802. The Order is the highest decoration in France and is divided into five degrees: Chevalier (Knight), Officier (Officer), Commandeur (Commander), Grand Officier (Grand Officer) and Grand Croix (Grand Cross).

Retrieved November 28, 2013 from http://en.wikipedia.org/wiki/L%C3%A9gion_d%27honne ur

In the luminosity of his theological writings, it is also forgotten that he was an eminent scientist, as Theodosius Dobzhansky, prominent geneticist and evolutionary biologist, writing in Chardin's *Letters to Two Friends* (1968) notes:

Between 1908 and 1949, Teilhard published sixty-seven major scientific papers on geology, between 1907 and 1952 a total of fifty-three papers on paleontology, and between 1913 and 1955 a total of thirty-nine papers of paleoanthropology. His complete bibliography amounts to some five hundred titles. His geological work covers a wide field; his studies on the geology of China stand out as a fundamental contribution to the understanding of the geological history of the heartland of Asia. As a paleontologist, Teilhard has concentrated his attention on the study of fossil mammals, again chiefly on those of China. A whole generation of Chinese geologists and paleontologists had him as one of their mentors and leaders. Together with

Davidson Black, W. C. Pei, and F. Weidenreich, Teilhard worked on the famous fossil remains discovered in the Chou-kou-tien locality near Peking, and named Peking Man (*Homo erectus pekinensis*). Teilhard was not the actual finder of the skull of this most ancient Prometheus (Peking Man is the earliest known user of fire), but his was nevertheless a key role, since he studied the geology of the locality and the associated fossil animals, making it thus possible to arrive at an approximate geological age of the Peking Man.

Teilhard's work as a research scientist brought him ample honors and recognition from his scientific colleagues. Among his other publications, *Early Man in China* (1941), *Chinese Fossil Mammals* (1942), *New Rodents of North China* (1942), *Le Neolithique de la Chine* (1944), *Les Felides de Chine* (1945), and *Les Mustelides de Chine* (1945) may especially be mentioned as having established his reputation. After his return from China to France in 1946, he was invited to become a candidate for a professorship at the College de France in Paris, one of the most prestigious positions to which a scientist can aspire in that country. His ecclesiastic superiors discouraged him from accepting this position; some of the letters in the present collection refer to this melancholy event, as well as to the still heavier blow that fell on him in 1950, when a permission to publish his major works (*Le Phenomene Humain* and *Le Groupe Zoologique Humain*) was withheld by the authorities in Rome. His greatest honor, election in 1950 to membership in the Academie des Sciences

(Institut de France), came however at about the same time. (pp. 223-224)

Perhaps one of the underlying reasons the writings of Fr. Teilhard were banned by the Vatican in 1962, may have been because his central thesis invalidated one of the central arguments long used by the Church in denying priestly ordination to women, the superiority of spirit over matter.

Halter (2004) explains:

> The *Didascalia Apostolorum* [Teaching of the Apostles, 3rd Century Syriac document] and the *Constitutiones Apostolicae* [Apostolic Constitution, 4th Century] were two examples of how gender-based dualism became fundamental to church thinking. According to this dualism, the body (matter, woman) was inferior to the head (mind, priest). To allow the body to "overtake" the head would "set aside the act of creation." In this scenario, the head needed the body to carry out its commands and could even act independently of the body, but the body could never have an idea or act on its own. (p. 49)

Teilhard de Chardin (1978) writes of his reflections on Matter which led him to realize its connection to Spirit:

> By its gravitational nature, the Universe, I saw, was falling—falling forwards—in the direction of Spirit as upon its stable form. In other words, Matter was not ultra-materialized as I would at first have believed, but was instead metamorphosed into Psyche. Looked at not metaphysically, but

genetically, Spirit was by no means the enemy or the opposite pole of the Tangibility which I was seeking to attain: rather was its very heart...

Meanwhile, my interior position was as follows. By the direct leap I had taken from the old static dualism, which I found paralyzing, to emerge into a Universe which was in a state not merely of evolution but of *directed evolution* (that is, of *Genesis*) I was obliged to make a complete about-turn in my fundamental pursuit of Consistence. Until that time, as I said earlier, my guiding Sense of Plentitude tended to point and settle down in the direction of the 'extremely simple' (in other words, of what cannot be broken down into physical components). In future, since the unique and precious essence of the Universe had assumed for me the form of an 'Evolutive' in which Matter was transformed into Thought as an extended consequence of Noogenesis, I found myself inevitably, and paradoxically, obliged to identify the extreme Solidity of things with *an extreme organic complexity*. Yet how could what was most corruptible become, as a result of synthesis, the supremely Indestructible? Because I had not yet perceived 'the biological laws of Union' and recognized the amazing attributes of a universal Curvature, I was still uncertain of the solution to that problem; but I no longer doubted but that the supreme happiness I had formerly looked for in 'Iron' was to be found only in Spirit. (Italics in original, p. 28)

Teaching of the Universal Christ as greater than the universe is a necessary teaching, as Chardin, *Science and Christ* (1965) writes:

> If the unbelievers are to begin to believe, and the believers to continue to do so, we must hold up before men the figure of the Universal Christ. (p. 15)

It is the same with the Universal Church and Women in the Church; if the Catholic Church is the Universal Church—though *how can it be* while subjugating women—how can unbelievers ever believe and believers continue to believe.

As the Church embraced the Mother Goddess of Mesoamerica, so the Church embraced pagan gods and their modern expressions: Freud/Jungian psychoanalysis, but all too often the Church has lost the passion, as Chardin (1975) notes:

> There is another idea which seems to me to be much more connected with the basic evolution of our thought. This (the most important basis of psychoanalysis) is that the energy which fuels our interior life and determines its fabric is in its primitive roots of a passionate nature. Like every other animal, man is essentially a tendency towards union that brings mutual completion; he is a capacity for loving, as Plato said long ago. It is from this primordial impulse that the luxuriant complexity of intellectual and emotional life develops and becomes more intense and diverse. For all their height and the breadth of their span, our spiritual ramifications have their roots deep in the corporeal. It is from man's storehouse of

passion that the warmth and light of his soul arise, transfigured. It is there, initially, that we hold concentrated, as in a seed, the finest essence, the most delicately adjusted spring, governing all spiritual development. (p. 68)

The Catholic Church, so long the center of education, has become the center of rules; so long the center of scientific creativity, has become stale; so long a center of ministry, has become the home of clericalism.

All of these are natural human tendencies, to regulate, to stagnate, to negate.

Fr. Teilhard shows us a different vision of evolutive learning on a Thomist foundation, embracing science and reason through the synthesis of spirit and matter.

God created all, but God's crowning creation is human beings—men *and* women—who, through their growth and evolution grow and evolve God.

The idea that God is within all, all matter and all spirit, is not a new idea, as St. Augustine (1993) wrote discussing Christians left unburied:

> And so there are indeed many bodies of Christians lying unburied; but no one has separated them from Heaven, nor from that earth which is all filled with the presence of Him who knows whence He will rise again what He created. (Book 1, 11, p. 17)

Criminal Reformation

I for one, have reached the conclusion that women should be priests and the continued closed-to-discussion stance of the popes seems to render much of what they are saying about other issues of Catholicism, much less important; and here is where we must come to a realization that, as important as it is to follow Peter, we must differentiate between Peter as he often acts in concert with the world's wishes and those of the club of priests, and Peter as he should act as the Vicar of Christ—welcoming all, causing no discrimination, except that based on sin, and even the priests cannot, in intellectual fairness, claim women, by their very nature are in sin—but that is what the current status of women in relation to not being allowed to become priests does in fact seem to proclaim.

How important is this to criminal reformation among Catholics in prison or outside of prison ministry?

Very important, because in the outside world, in the United States, women are generally acknowledged as equal to men in all things, even now it is being easily considered that a woman will soon become president.

With this reality in the world and with the reality that in the professional criminal world, women have held roughly equal stature for many years, seeing how women in the Catholic Church are not permitted to do what the men can, and seeing that the reasons given are logically weak, well, that will just not do, that will create a problem, with them, as it has with me; and whether it is ten or so years after baptism, as it has been with me, the impact will be the same; a weakening of faith in the authority of the institutional Church.

An important point concerns the times and social circumstances in which certain practices originated versus the times and social circumstances in which they are challenged, which Rahner (1992) addressed when writing about the *Declaration on the Question of the Admission of Women to the Ministerial Priesthood,* of October 15, 1976 by the Congregation for the Doctrine of the Faith and approved by Pope Paul VI:

> We come finally to the crucial point in the argumentation of the Roman declaration. Once more a preliminary observation must be made. A practical rule of action can be culturally and sociologically conditioned and be open to change, and actually change, as a result of a changed cultural and sociological situation, and yet at an earlier stage may not only have existed and been sociologically recognized, but may even have been "objectively" opposed to more general and more fundamental moral principles also recognized and affirmed at the time, but not then seen or only slowly seen clearly as opposed in the consciousness of a society. As a result the more general principle only slowly changed the situation in that society and made it aware of a new and more concrete rule of action, although previously a contrary rule not only existed in fact but was at the time morally permitted or even binding, since it was impossible or only possible by immoral violence to change the sociological situation from which it had emerged.
>
> This fundamental consideration certainly does not need to be supported by examples or substantiated in principle. If someone wants examples, he has only to recall the institution of slavery during the

first Christian centuries, polygamy in the Old Testament, the laws of war in the Old Testament, or the church's prohibition of usury until well into the eighteenth century. In all these cases it is decisively important to observe that a concrete rule of action coexisted with more general moral principles, while being really "in the abstract" opposed to the latter, although this basic contradiction could not in practice be perceived in the earlier sociological situation. Hence this particular rule of action could be permitted, with things being thus, and even be required, thus slowing down change in the situation on which it depended. (pp. 427-428)

Criminals, usually quite conscious of the meaning of sociobiological conditions determining theological principles, will tend to agree with this argument by Fr. Karl Rahner, S.J., one of the foremost theologians of the 20th Century and who played a large role in Vatican II, as Wikipedia notes:

Karl Rahner, SJ (March 5, 1904 – March 30, 1984), was a German Jesuit priest and theologian who, alongside Henri de Lubac, Hans Urs von Balthasar, and Yves Congar, is considered one of the most influential Catholic theologians of the 20th century...

Before the Second Vatican Council, Rahner had worked alongside Yves Congar, Henri de Lubac and Marie-Dominique Chenu, theologians associated with an emerging school of thought called the Nouvelle Théologie, elements of which had been condemned in the encyclical *Humani Generis* of Pope Pius XII. Subsequently, however, the Second

Vatican Council was much influenced by his theology and his understanding of Catholic faith. (n.p.) Retrieved May 28, 2014 from http://en.wikipedia.org/wiki/Karl_Rahner

I've mentioned it before, but it can't be said enough; the theologians who support women's ordination have been making excellent arguments—better than those of the Vatican—for decades now.

Rahner (1992) again:

> If however the assumptions stated above and the methodical considerations likewise merely indicated can be recognized, then the conclusion seems inescapable that the attitude of Jesus and his apostles is sufficiently explained by the cultural and sociological milieu in which they acted and had to act as they did, while their behavior did not need to have a normative significance for all times—that is, for the time when this cultural and social milieu had been substantially changed. It does not seem to be proved that the actual behavior of Jesus and the apostles implies a norm of divine revelation in the strict sense of the term. This practice (even if it existed for a long time and without being questioned) can certainly be understood as "human" tradition like other traditions in the church which were once unquestioned, had existed for a long time, and nevertheless became obsolete as a result of a sociological and cultural change. (p. 430)

Concerning the current sociological conditions, Pew Research Center (2013, March 13-17) recently polled Catholics and 59% want women to become priests:

> The latest national survey by the Pew Research Center, conducted March 13-17 among 1,501 adults (including 325 Catholics), also finds that majorities of Catholics want the church to change some of its teachings and policies. Three-quarters of Catholics (76%), for example, say the church should allow Catholics to use birth control. Nearly two-thirds of Catholics (64%) say that priests should be allowed to get married, and six-in-ten (59%) endorse the idea of allowing women to become priests. (n.p.)

Criminal reformation includes understanding the personhood of women in opposition to the lust-drunk siren song of male fantasy, magnified within the criminal/carceral world to dangerous and outlandish levels; though tempered by the normative association within the criminal life with entrepreneurial women in the thievery, sex work, drug sales, and other activities of the professional criminal.

The woman saint that professional criminals most relate to is certainly St. Mary Magdalene, for, according to the ancient tradition in the Church, she too was a professional criminal, and she too was loved by Christ, who chose her to witness his resurrection before all others and, as 'apostle to the apostles' then take that history shattering—nothing would ever again be the same—news to the twelve.

In relation to Teilhard's expansion of Johannine theology of the drawing "of all men to myself" (John 12:32), Pope

Emeritus Benedict (2004) makes a crucial connection in relation to criminal reformation:

> In the human dream of a perfect world, holiness is always visualized as untouchability by sin and evil, as something unmixed with the latter; there always remains in some form or other a tendency to think in terms of black and white, a tendency to shut out and reject mercilessly the current form of the negative (which can be conceived in widely varying terms). In contemporary criticism of society and in the actions in which it vents itself, this relentless side always present in human ideals is once again only too evident. That is why the aspect of Christ's holiness that upset his contemporaries was the complete absence of this condemnatory note—fire did not fall on the unworthy, nor were the zealous allowed to pull up the weeds they saw growing luxuriantly on all sides. On the contrary, this holiness expressed itself precisely as mingling with the sinners whom Jesus drew into his vicinity; as mingling to the point where he himself was made "to be sin" and bore the curse of the law in execution as a criminal—complete community of faith with the lost. He has drawn sin to himself, made it his lot, and so revealed what true "holiness" is: not separation, but union; not judgment, but redeeming love. (p. 342)

Within this lies the root of why only the reformed criminal can reform criminals; and, of course, even better, those few and so rare Catholics who possess a deep and saintly Christological interiority.

St. Catherine of Siena

St. Catherine lived a youthful life opposite that of Magdalene—whose youth was one of debauchery—rather spending it in prayer and service, as Gardner (2009) writes:

> She was only six years old when she returned with her brother Stefano from the house of their sister Bonaventura, looked up, and saw over the summit of the church of San Domenico, Christ seated on an imperial throne, clad in the papal robes and wearing a tiara, attended by Sts. Peter and Paul and the beloved disciple, John. He smiled upon her and blessed her, and she was absorbed in ecstasy. She didn't know where she was until her brother, calling and pulling her by the hand, brought her back to Earth.
>
> It was at this time that Catherine became more silent, and she began to abstain from food and to afflict her own flesh. She wandered in the woods and caves in order to imitate the ancient anchorites of the desert. She dreamed of entering the Dominican Order in the disguise of a boy. She gathered other little girls of the same age around her, to join in her prayers and discipline themselves together with her. Burning more and more with the fire of divine love every day, she consecrated her virginity to Christ. In later years, she told her confessors that all of this happened when she was only seven. (pp. 17-18)

It is difficult to imagine a life like this today, when the distractions of our technological age, especially for the young, fill our days, generally excluding such rarefied spiritual events as Catherine experienced.

It is so appropriate that Catherine grew within the embrace of the Dominicans (another Doctor of the Church, St. Thomas Aquinas, was a Dominican) becoming a member of the Third Order of the Dominicans, the Sisters of Penance of St. Dominic, through her own exhortation.

Gardner explains:

> At first, the Sisters refused to receive a maiden into their number, as their order was then composed only of widows, but after a while, when Catherine lay ill and assured her mother that God and St. Dominic would take her from the world if her desire was not fulfilled, they told Lapa they would accept Catherine, provided that the girl was not too beautiful. They accepted her as a Sister, and on her recovery to health, she received the habit from one of the Dominican Friars who acted as director of the sisterhood at San Domenico in the Cappella delle Volte—that little chapel still so fragrant with her spirit. There is some small difference of opinion as to the date of her taking the habit, but I think it was about the beginning of 1363. (*Ibid.* pp. 20-21)

Aquinas, the Angelic Doctor, and also an Italian Dominican, died March 7, 1274, seventy three years before she was born, March 25, 1347, and twenty four years before she was born, in 1323, Thomas was declared a saint.

These were very important times for the Church and few women, nor men for that matter, played a role as important as Catherine, noted by Frugoni (1992):

Catherine of Siena (1347-1380), a Dominican tertiary who was an interlocutor of Pope Gregory XI, was awarded nothing less than the triple halo and crown. In addition to being a virgin and a martyr, for her uncomplaining suffering and vanquished temptations, she was also a "preacher," annulling Saint Paul's prohibition against women speaking in public. Her two biographers, Raimondo of Capua and Tommaso di Antonio of Siena (better known as the "Caffarini"), stressed in particular the authenticity of Saint Catherine's prophetic mission together with the elevated level of her doctrine. Analogies were drawn between her and Saint John, who preached glad tidings and wrote everything down in the Gospel. (pp. 417-418)

Simone de Beauvoir (2010) in her magisterial work on women writes of Catherine's importance in relation to other women in the Middle Ages:

Joan of Arc's adventure is something of a miracle; and it is, moreover, a very brief adventure. But Saint Catherine of Siena's story is meaningful; she creates a great reputation in Siena for charitable activity and for the visions that testify to her intense inner life within a very normal existence; she thus acquires the necessary authority for success generally lacking in women; her influence is invoked to hearten those condemned to death, to bring back to the fold those who were lost, to appease quarrels between families and towns. She is supported by the community that recognizes itself in her, which is how she is able to fulfill her pacifying mission, preaching submission to the pope from city to city, carrying on a vast correspondence with bishops and sovereigns, and finally chosen by Florence as ambassador to go and find the pope in Avignon. Queens, by divine right, and saints, by their shining virtues, are assured of support in the society that allows them to be men's equal. Of others, a silent modesty is required. (p. 115)

And again:

Catherine of Siena and Saint Teresa are saintly souls, beyond any physiological condition; their lay life and their mystical life, their actions and their writings, rise to heights that few men ever attain. (*Ibid.* p. 150)

Beauvoir also writes about the historic strength of the women of Siena:

To defend their city against Montluc, Sienese women marshalled three thousand female troop commanded by women. (*Ibid.* pp. 117-118)

Conclusion

For many years after baptism I was scornful of cafeteria Catholics who picked the doctrines they chose to believe and ignored the rest; however, beginning with the Church's dealing with capital punishment—where 2,000 years of teaching support its use, but recent popes and virtually all bishops now support calls for its abolition—I realized that a properly formed conscience, based on in-depth study of Church history and teaching, can justify the cafeteria approach.

This became validated once I began studying the issue of women's ordination where the reasons given for it not being allowed were theologically weak and rationally unsound—so much so that the Holy Father now claimed it was not even open to discussion anymore; this after preceding popes and Curia organizations had discussed it at length.

And here is where the concept of the People of God comes into play. Before Christ there was Judaism, the religion of God's Chosen People. After Christ came Catholicism and just as the Pharisees corrupted Judaism, so has the Vatican corrupted Catholicism; yet one appellation remains constant—the People of God, Jews and Catholics.

The tabernacle, the sanctuary, the synagogue, is in the humble heart of the people, who do not say, follow me for I know the truth; but they pray to God to help them live a life of truth, a life *they know* is governed by the Great Law: 'Love God and Neighbor'.

There are two covenants within Judaism/Catholicism; the Old and the New. The Old is Judaism, the new is Catholicism, but they are two sides of the same coin, we are brothers and sisters in faith. We are God's Chosen People, we are the People of God.

Israel is the home of our faith; Rome is the center of governance.

Liberal/Conservative, Traditional/Cafeteria, these are handy labels, but they only have meaning in relation to our stand on issues. If we follow our conscience regarding Catholic praxis, our conscience must be informed, we must study, pray, reflect and reach conclusions only after we have done the work; accepting that in the future, we may learn more and change our conclusions.

I think it was Walt Whitman who said regarding this, "I embrace my contradictions", or something to that effect.

Underlying any discussion about women in the priesthood or the broad acceptance of spiritual/material evolutionary theory as put forward by Teilhard de Chardin, is the resistance of large institutions, like the Roman Catholic Church, to change; something Noonan (2005) is particularly eloquent about:

> The deepest resistance to change may arise at the vital core of the resister. Life certainties are being disturbed. The resister has staked his or her salvation on the truth of certain religious propositions and on the impossibility of error in any one of them. It is unbearable that any of these propositions should fall into doubt, desuetude, or

repudiation. Analogy again is agonizing. If this one goes, why not that one? The resister's rock will become a mound of broken boulders. Better to shut one's eyes, better to cling to the old fortifications, than let anything be displaced. The impulse comes from the heart. The human heart hungers for certainty about the human person's destiny after death. Danger lies in any religious truth being open to development. Development may dissolve doctrine at its core. Change has to be fought lest the whole edifice of belief crumble.

We can recognize this existential dread. All of us share it. Recognition and sharing do not release us from confronting change when change has occurred. But the greatest obstacle to acknowledging that change has occurred is what appears as a concomitant of the acknowledgement: the admission of error. Could the Church actually have been wrong on a moral question? *Absit!* many a theologian would have cried. The disinclination to recognize the possibility ignores the infallibility with which the Church is endowed. The infallibility is true of teaching within strictly defined limits. Those limits must be respected. More importantly, the implication of infallibility must be drawn. If the Church is infallible only under certain specified conditions, the Church is fallible the rest of the time. The doctrine of infallibility is an invitation neither to dogmatism nor skepticism, but to the admission of mistakes where the rest of the time they may have been made.

It may be said that the Church will lose moral authority by acknowledging error in its moral teaching. Who will trust a guide that admits mistakes? Fear of this question often dogs authority. It may be answered by three analogies, none of the situations exactly the same as that of the Church, but close enough to be helpful. Do parents lose or gain authority with their children when they admit to a mistake in guiding them? For modern children, the parents' candor enhances respect for their parents' wisdom and loving care. Does a judicial system gain or lose authority by admitting errors? In the United States an elaborate system of appeals has been set up to correct errors by courts, with state courts sometimes subjected to additional correction by federal courts; it is assumed that error may occur. The Supreme Court itself often reverses its views on the constitution, finding its earlier reading of the text erroneous. Yet nowhere, it may be guessed, is the prestige of a judicial system higher than in the United States. Finally, the modern scientific enterprise is built on the assumption that any conclusion is open to challenge and correction; answers are always tentative, hypothetical, subject to refutation or revision. Yet scientific knowledge is probably the most highly prized secular knowledge that the present world possesses. Admitting error, the Church would not fare worse than parents, judges, or scientists, except perhaps among those who have conceived of the magisterium as a perfect machine perfectly enunciating moral truth in all ways at all times in all places. (pp. 195-196)

This is such a clear statement of the quandary the institutional Church finds itself in regarding women's ordination, but feeling the 'perfect machine' must be protected is proving much more disastrous to the Church than admitting mistakes; and not only with this issue, but also, as we have seen, with the issue of sexual abuse of children by priests and bishops.

There are now women—including religious—in the Church whose major reason for staying in the Church is to struggle against the 'perfect machine', to change it from within; and their number will change dramatically once women are priests and join the true ordained leadership of Holy Mother Church.

Many of these women are working within base communities, which are noted by Conmy (2013, March 5) in a post discussing a meeting in Rome:

> During our meeting we took a drive across town to the San Paolo Base Community, one of four "Basic Christian Communities" in Rome. From their founding documents, they are "engaged in overcoming the contradiction between the Spirit of the Gospel, and the practice of the Roman Catholic institution." These communities formed organically in the 1960s and 70s throughout Latin America and Italy "not to create another Church," but to help include "the other" in the Roman Catholic Church. (n.p.)

Unfortunately, "the other" still includes women.

There are a group of Catholic theologians and writers who have connected themselves to the work of Fr. Teilhard, claiming to be his inheritors, but it is an inherited connection only having validity with folks unfamiliar with Teilhard or willfully misreading him; for this group of theologians and writers are essentially writing about a New Age vision of the future with specific warnings about protecting the ecology from the evil capitalists, a political reading Teilhard did not appear to even consider.

These theologians and writers speak from the perspective that human beings are merely a part of creation while Teilhard, reflecting his Catholic beliefs, knows humans are the pinnacle of creation, the virtual, evolving mind of Christ as he draws all to him, the human mind and experiences—co-creating with God—form the primary ingredient of the future of humans.

These theologian and writers, tend to see human beings as a cancer upon the earth; they are deep ecologists, generally Gaia adherents, primitives, who believe that all of the technological work humans do to use earth's resources to make human life safer, longer, more productive, and more comfortable, is a rape of the earth, rather than what it truly is, the right use of the gifts of creation.

To Teilhard, God was the Cosmic Christ who, having risen draws everything to him, rooted in Paul's theology. To those for whom God is Gaia—rooted in primitive earth/animal worship, coming from pre-Christian, pagan visions, their thought, whether they know it or not, is ultimately Satanic.

The Pontifical Council for Culture (2003) describes the New Age perception of God:

> New Age has a marked preference for Eastern or pre-Christian religions, which are reckoned to be uncontaminated by Judeo-Christian distortions. Hence great respect is given to ancient agricultural

rites and to fertility cults. "Gaia", Mother Earth, is offered as an alternative to God the Father, whose image is seen to be linked to a patriarchal conception of male domination of women. There is talk of God, but it is not a personal God; the God of which New Age speaks is neither personal nor transcendent. Nor is it the Creator and sustainer of the universe, but an "impersonal energy" immanent in the world, with which it forms a "cosmic unity": "All is one". This unity is monistic, pantheistic or, more precisely, panentheistic. God is the "life-principle", the "spirit or soul of the world", the sum total of consciousness existing in the world. In a sense, everything is God. God's presence is clearest in the spiritual aspects of reality, so every mind/spirit is, in some sense, God. (Section 2.3.4.2. ...God?)

While it is easy to see how this New Age perspective can be conflated with the work of Fr. Teilhard, the conflation is a result of laziness and a lack of deep study of Teilhard.

However, a call from some Catholic women theologians to develop a "Magdalene function" within ecclesiology *is crucial* if the Church is to move further, as Hinsdale (2011) writes:

> My presenting question in this address was to ask, "what would ecclesiology look like if we started with biblical materials which feature the witness of Mary of Magdala?" Could a "Magdalene function," similar to the "Petrine function" agreed upon so many years ago in ecumenical dialogue, be more fruitful in recognizing the prophetic and apostolic leadership roles of women in the church today?

As we have seen, recent biblical scholarship attests to an apostolic role given to Mary Magdalene within the canonical texts. Feminist hermeneutics of suspicion in particular sheds light on the suppression of women's leadership roles in the early church, even within the New Testament. When non-canonical materials are investigated employing a hermeneutic of remembrance, we find further evidence of material inspired by the memory of Mary Magdalene. This material could achieve greater relevance for ecclesiology in recovering a "Magdalene function" if not only canonical texts, but the whole range of material, including apocryphal Gospels and even the legends which fueled popular beliefs about her would be critically re-considered, since all of them contribute to a long historical "tradition" about Mary Magdalene. (pp. 82-83)

The answer to her presenting question is, of course, a very robust Yes!

Remember, remember, as Hinsdale (2006) reminds us:

...before Sister Madeleva Wolff's School of Sacred Theology was begun in 1943 (only a little more than sixty years ago!), nowhere in the United States could a woman earn a PhD in theology. (p. 7)

We desperately need more work on this and fortunately, now, there are a great many Catholic women theologians working on issues related to women in the Church and as they mature and deepen in the theological studies men have been toiling in for hundreds of years, we, and the Church, will benefit from their work.

We all need—in partnership with these theologians—to ask the Catholic Church to release women from 2,000 years of clerical bondage, seek forgiveness from them 70 times 7 times, and welcome them, finally, into the work God intends for them, as priests, bishops, and popes, in partnership with men in the saving of souls and building the eternal cathedral of the Church in the world and in heaven.

The Church must embrace its full moral power by ordaining women—power-with the Russian Orthodox as it struggles to emerge from domination by Communism—as the great re-unification becomes possible, for Russia is crucial, as Fatima taught us, and as Soloviev (2013) writing in the 19th Century understood:

> The profoundly religious and monarchic instinct of the Russian people, certain prophetic events in its past history, the enormous and compact bulk of its Empire, the great latent strength of the national spirit in contrast to the poverty and emptiness of its actual existence—all this seems to indicate that it is the historic destiny of Russia to provide the Universal Church with the political power which it requires for the salvation and regeneration of Europe and of the world. (pp. 26-27)

Perhaps, as Catherine of Siena so long ago brought the pope back from France to Rome, it will be a woman priest, bishop, or pope, who will lead the joining of the two great lungs of the Church, Russia and Rome, together again.

St. Catherine (1980) the great mystic, was also a magnificent political strategist, who, in the 14th century, focused:

...her attention to her larger concerns: the crusade, the reform of the clergy, the return of the papacy to Rome. (p. 6)

Pope Gregory XI did return to Rome and she:

...certainly influenced the actual move. (*Ibid.* p. 6)

Russia has, for centuries, reached for internal unity and, in a reminder from Soloviev (2013) writing in the 19th century, that history lives today:

> For centuries, the history of our country was moving toward a single objective, the formation of a great national monarchy. The union of Ukraine and a part of White Russia with Muscovite Russia under the Tsar Alexis was a decisive moment in this historic work; for that union put an end to the dispute for primacy between the Russia of the North and that of the South, between Moscow and Kiev, and gave a real meaning to the title of "Tsar of all the Russias." (p. 40)

And now, after the fall of the USSR, Russia rises again—grasping Ukraine once more to its bosom, and we see the formation of the first Orthodox Council in over a thousand years being discussed, as reported by Pentin (2014, April 3):

> Where does the Russian Orthodox Church stand on the crisis in Ukraine? And why is a Pan-Orthodox Council planned for 2016?
>
> To find out answers to these and other questions, the Register interviewed Metropolitan Hilarion

Alfeyev of Volokolamsk, the chairman of the Department of External Church Relations of the Russian Orthodox Church and a permanent member of the Holy Synod of the Patriarchate of Moscow.

A noted theologian, Church historian and composer, Metropolitan Hilarion also shared in this April 2 email interview his thoughts on the current status of Catholic-Orthodox relations.

How important for the Orthodox Church is the Pan-Orthodox Council planned for 2016? Is it to be seen as something similar to Vatican II in the history of the Catholic Church?

The Pan-Orthodox Council is important in that, after the era of ecumenical councils, it will be the first council representing all the Orthodox Churches recognized today. For the last 12 centuries, there were councils of various levels attended by representatives of various Churches, but this one will be the first Pan-Orthodox Council to be convened in this period.

This council is a fruit of long work carried out by local Orthodox Churches for over 50 years. It is hardly appropriate to compare it with Vatican II, because their agendas are utterly different. Besides, we do not expect it to introduce any reforms making a substantial impact on the life of Orthodoxy.

Patriarch Kirill said that the Pan-Orthodox Council should deal with such issues as the expulsion of Christians from the Middle East and North Africa, the cult of consumerism, the destruction of the moral foundations and the family, cloning and surrogate motherhood. How important are these issues for you, and would you also like other themes, such as unity with the Catholic Church, included in the council's agenda?

These statements by His Holiness Patriarch Kirill reflect the position of the Russian Orthodox Church, whereby the Pan-Orthodox Council's agenda needs to be supplemented with themes topical for today's society and requiring a response from the world Orthodoxy. Besides, there is a list of 10 themes on which documents have been drafted by the local Orthodox Churches during the many years of preparatory pre-council work. All Orthodox Churches have already reached unanimity on eight of them, and, after some improvement, these documents will be submitted to the council. Among them is also the theme of the Orthodox Church's attitude to the continuation of dialogue with other Christian confessions, including Catholicism. (n.p.)

Should, could, this Council lead to unity? What a glorious day that would be.

In a larger sense, a glorious day is already upon us, foretold by Teilhard de Chardin (1964), where he writes:

From the first beginnings of History, let me repeat, this principle of the compressive generation of consciousness has been ceaselessly at work in the human mass. But from the moment — we have just reached it! — when the compression of populations in the teeming continents gains a decided ascendancy over their movement of expansion upon the earth's surface, the process is naturally speeded up to a staggering extent. We are today witnessing a truly explosive growth of technology and research, bringing and increasing mastery, both theoretical and practical, of the secrets and sources of cosmic energy at every level and in every form; and, correlative with this, the rapid heightening of what I have called the psychic temperature of the earth. A single glance at the overall picture of surface chaos is enough to assure us that this is so. We see a human tide bearing us upward with all the force of a contracting star; not a spreading tide, as we might suppose, but one that is rising: the ineluctable growth on our horizon of a true state of 'ultra-humanity'. (pp. 275-276)

What we are now part of, through the noosphere, the power of the Mystical Church, and the opening wide the anciently narrow Catholic Gate, is conscious evolution, which because God began it has always been conscious, but now human beings are part of it:

It may be said that for a long time, under pressure of the external forces engaged in concentrating it, the Human developed in a fashion that was mainly automatic—spurred on principally, in Bergson's expression, by a *vis a tergo*, a 'push from behind.' But when intelligence, which originally, as has been well said, was simply a means of survival, became gradually elevated to the function and dignity of 'a reason for living', it was inevitable that, with the accentuation of the forces of free will, a profound modification should become discernible in the

113

working of anthropogenesis, and one of which we are only now beginning to experience the full effects. No doubt it is true that certain inward necessities, persisting in the most spiritualized recesses of our being, inexorably compel us to continue our forward progress. What power on earth has ever succeeded in arresting the growth of an idea or a passion, once they have taken shape? But the fact remains that, as Reflection increases, there is added and allied to this basic determinism the possibility of Man's withdrawal or rejection of whatever does not appear to satisfy his heart or his reason. Which is to say, that given a sufficient degree of hominisation, the 'planetary sequence' generating the Human can only continue to operate in an atmosphere of *consent*—meaning, finally, under the impulsion of some desire. So that in line with, and gradually replacing, the thrust from behind or below, we see the appearance of a force of attraction coming from above which shows itself to be organically indispensable for the continuation of the sequence, indispensable for the maintenance of the evolutionary impetus, and also indispensable for the creation of an atmosphere enveloping Mankind in the process of totalisation, of psychic warmth and kindness without which Man's economic-technological grip upon the World can only crush souls together, without causing them to fuse and unite...The 'pull' after the 'push' as the English would say. (*Ibid.* pp. 276-277)

With this being foretold and now playing itself out in the wired world, and with recent popes noting the importance of Fr. Teilhard's work; it is sad to see the struggle between the Vatican's Congregation for the Doctrine of the Faith

(CDF), and the Leadership Conference of Women Religious (LCWR) currently (May 2014) arguing over the calling of a conference speaker whose past authorship of a book on conscious evolution and who claims a deep indebtedness to Fr. Teilhard, seems to be an issue, as reported by Carey (2014, May 5):

> Cardinal Müller explained that, for the last several years, the CDF has been concerned about the LCWR focusing attention on the concept of conscious evolution. He said that since Barbara Marx Hubbard addressed the 2012 LCWR assembly on the topic, every issue of the LCWR newsletter has discussed conscious evolution in some way. "We have even seen some religious institutes modify their directional statements to incorporate concepts and undeveloped terms from conscious evolution," he added.

> Apologizing for sounding blunt, the cardinal continued: "The fundamental theses of conscious evolution are opposed to Christian Revelation and, when taken unreflectively, lead almost necessarily to fundamental errors regarding the omnipotence of God, the incarnation of Christ, the reality of Original Sin, the necessity of salvation and the definitive nature of the salvific action of Christ in the Paschal Mystery." (n.p.)

I think the key words here are "when taken unreflectively" as all too many of those who dabble in such esoteric ideas as conscious evolution, do not do so in a scholarly way or through the delving into the primary sources like Fr. Teilhard, but rely too much on the works produced by the populaizers of these ideas, which all too often, come out in New Age jargon.

As part of the kerfuffle around the LCWR with the Vatican, is the theology of this speaker on "conscious evolution"; which the LCWR has speak at their conferences, who says she was influenced by Fr. Pierre Teilhard de Chardin; joining many other theologians—Catholic and not—who also claim a spiritual mentorship from Teilhard.

What is unfortunate about this is that it tends to keep many Catholics from exploring the work of Fr. Teilhard, whose work recent popes have clearly stated is worth exploring; even though Fr. Teilhard was refused permission to publish his works during his lifetime.

The signature difference between many of the theologians—Catholic or not—who claim a connection with Teilhard and Teilhard himself, is that Fr. Teilhard was a true son of the Church and his work was always centered on Christ; whereas most of the new theologian's work claiming connection to him seems to be more connected to recent scripts from Star Wars and Hobbit movies than from him.

The same thing has happened with Pope Francis, as taking many of his statements out of context and building them into a virtual rejection of Catholic teaching rather than the deep expansion of it that actually lies at the core of our Holy Father's work, another Jesuit and true son of the Church.

As someone who has studied Fr. Teilhard's work for many years and still finding myself amazed at the depth and prophetic reach of this great Jesuit, I feel certain that someday he will be fully recognized for what he is, a saint and Doctor of the Church.

Here is a website listing the complete works of Fr. Teilhard, http://teilharddechardin.org/index.php/teilhards-publications

I have accumulated all of these listed works over the years and they represent a lifetime of future study, which I propose, any Catholic would be richly rewarded by pursuing.

Here is one excerpt from Chardin (1978) which so beautifully captures his evolutionary thought and theological reflection:

> In a sense, Christ is in the Church in the same way as the sun is before our eyes. We see the same sun as our fathers saw, and yet we understand it in a much more magnificent way. I believe the Church is still a child. Christ, by whom she lives, is immeasurably greater than she imagines. And yet, when thousands of years have gone by and Christ's true countenance is a little more plainly seen, the Christians of those days will still, without any reservations, recite the Apostles' Creed. (pp. 117-118) Written by Fr. Teilhard on January 5, 1921.

The Apostles' Creed (each of the 12 apostles was believed to have contributed a line):

1. I believe in God the Father almighty, creator of heaven and earth.
2. I believe in Jesus Christ, his only Son, our Lord.

3. He was conceived by the power of the Holy Spirit and born of the Virgin Mary.

4. Under Pontius Pilate, He was crucified, died, and was buried.

5. He descended to the dead. On the third day he rose again.

6. He ascended into heaven and is seated at the right hand of the Father.

7. He will come again to judge the living and the dead.

8. I believe in the Holy Spirit,

9. the holy catholic Church, the communion of saints,

10. the forgiveness of sins,

11. the resurrection of the body,

12. and the life everlasting.

Amen.

Christ says in John 12:32:

> **[31]** Now is the judgment of the world: now shall the prince of this world be cast out. **[32]** And I, if I be lifted up from the earth, will draw all things to myself.

Teilhard's concept of evolution in Christ is built upon this, for if evolution is true, and Teilhard, as a scientist, knew that it is; and if Christ is true, and Teilhard as a Jesuit and son of the Church, knew that he is, then Christ is at the center of and animating evolution.

Teilhard de Chardin (1971) knew that understanding this was crucial to the Church:

> My profound conviction, born of the experience of a life spent simultaneously in the heart of the Gentile world and in that of the Church, is that at this very

moment, we have reached a delicate point of balance at which a readjustment is essential. It could not, in fact, be otherwise: our Christology is still expressed in exactly the same terms as those which, three centuries ago, could satisfy men whose outlook on the cosmos is not physically impossible for us to accept. Unless we admit that religious life and human life are independent of one another (which is a psychological impossibility) such a situation must *a priori* produce a feeling of dismay, a loss of balance. That it has already done so cannot be denied. I can testify to this in my own case, and the whole of what we call the modernist movement bears me out. What we now have to do without delay is to modify the position occupied by the central core of Christianity—and this precisely in order that it may not lose its illuminative value.

If we ask in what exactly this correction in *relationship* consists, the answer must be in bringing Christology and evolution into line with one another. (p. 77)

This call to bring into alignment science and faith was part of the impetus for Vatican II, and much good has come from that council, but there are still central aspects that have not, and the status of women in the Church still reeks of centuries-old ideas which have indeed, caused the Church to lose some of "its illuminative value."

Finally, Rahner (1992) points the way forward, ever forward:

The Roman declaration [*Declaration on the Question of the Admission of Women to the*

Ministerial Priesthood, of October 15, 1976 by the Congregation for the Doctrine of the Faith and approved by Pope Paul VI] says that in this question the church must remain faithful to Jesus Christ. This is of course true in principle. But what fidelity means in connection with this problem remains an open question. Consequently, the discussion must continue. Cautiously, with mutual respect, critical of bad arguments on both sides, critical of irrelevant emotionalism expressively or tacitly influencing both sides, but also with that courage for historical change with is part of the fidelity which the church owes to its Lord. (p. 433)

After ten years as a Catholic, ten years of constant study of the theology and praxis of the Church, the theology stands radiant and sure, but the praxis suffers from contradiction, unreasonableness, and even, I am sad to say, harmfulness.

For the first eight or so years of being Catholic, my study remained in orthodox fields, but once praxis cracks opened up allowing a more subtle light to enter, I ventured into the writings of the unorthodox and even those sanctioned by the Church, writing from the perspective of the woman's ordination movement.

I studied scriptures, not only the canonical, but the non-canonical and the gnostic.

The world thus opened up to me posed no threat to the essential theology of the Church represented by her ancient creed, which still, and always will, hold my heart within its bond:

I believe in God, the Father Almighty, Creator of heaven and earth, and in Jesus Christ, his only son, our Lord; who was conceived by the Holy Spirit, born of the Virgin Mary, suffered under Pontius Pilate, was crucified, died and was buried; he descended into hell; on the third day he rose again from the dead, and is seated at the right hand of God the Father Almighty; from there he will come to judge the living and the dead. I believe in the Holy Spirit, the holy Catholic Church, the communion of Saints, the forgiveness of sins, the resurrection of the body, and life everlasting. Amen.

Yes, the Catholic Church on earth has been and is now, corrupted by the works of men; but her supernatural, eternal reality: the communion of saints, the deep holiness of so many of her popes—Pius XII stands so clear to me as an example within memory of what is great and holy about Peter—is not corrupted nor can it ever be; and yet, the earthly, corrupted, and pilgrim Catholic Church, is still the widest and most illuminated of the many narrow gates to heaven.

References

Augustine, S. ((1993). *The city of God*. New York: The Modern Library.

Beard, M. (2014, February 14). The Public Voice of Women. *London Review of Books*. Retrieved March 10, 2014 from http://www.lrb.co.uk/2014/02/14/mary-beard/the-public-voice-of-women

Boff, L. (1987). *The maternal face of God: The feminine and its religious expressions*. (Trans. R. R. Barr & J. W. Diercksmeier). San Francisco: Harper & Row, Publishers.

Beauvoir, S.D. (2010). *The second sex*. New York: Alfred A. Knopf.

Brock, A. G. (2003). *Mary Magdalene, the first apostle: The struggle for authority*. Cambridge, Massachusetts: Harvard University Press.

Campbell, J. (1988). *The power of myth: With Bill Moyers*. (Flowers, B. S., Ed.) New York: Doubleday.

Carey, A. (2014, May 5). Cardinal Müller: LCWR Stands in 'Open Provocation' of Holy See, *National Catholic Register*. Retrieved May 6, 2014 from http://www.ncregister.com/daily-news/cardinal-mueller-lcwr-stands-in-open-provocation-of-holy-see/

Carter, J. (2014). *A call to action: Women, religion, violence, and power*. New York: Simon & Schuster.

Catechism of the Catholic Church, (1994). United States Catholic Conference, Inc.—Liberia Editrice Vaticana. San Francisco: Ignatius Press.

Catherine of Siena (1980). *The dialogue*. (S. Noffke, *Trans*.) New York: Paulist Press.

Catherine of Siena. (2000). *The letters of Catherine of Siena*: Volume 1. (S. Noffke, O. P., Trans.) Tempe, Arizona: Arizona Center for Medieval and Renaissance Studies.

Catholic World News. (2014, January 20). *Former Swiss Guard commander confirms 'gay lobby' at Vatican.* Retrieved January 23, 2014 from http://www.catholicculture.org/news/headlines/index.cfm ?storyid=20241

Chardin, P. T. D. (1964). *The future of man*. (Trans. N. Denny). New York: Harper & Row, Publishers.

Chardin, P.T.D. (1965). *The making of a mind: Letters from a soldier-priest 1914-1919*. (Trans. R. Hague). St. James Place, London: Collins.

Chardin, P.T.D. (1965). *Science and Christ*. (Trans. R. Hague). New York: Harper & Row, Publishers.

Chardin, P.T.D. (1968). *Letters to two friends: 1926-1952*. (Trans. H. Weaver) New York: The New American Library.

Chardin, P.T.D. (1971). *Christianity and evolution*. (Trans. R. Hague). New York: A Helen and Kurt Wolff Book, Harcourt Brace Jovanovich, Inc.

Chardin, P. T. D. (1975). *Toward the future.* (Trans. R. Hague). New York: A Helen and Kurt Wolff Book, Harcourt Brace Jovanovich.

Chardin, P. T. D. (1978). *The heart of matter.* (. Trans. R. Hague). New York: A Helen and Kurt Wolff Book, Harcourt Brace Jovanovich.

Chardin, P.T.D. (2003). *The human phenomena.* (Trans. S. Appleton-Weber). Brighton: Sussex Academic Press.

Conmy, K. (2014, March 5). Base communities and the invisible. *The table: WOC blog.* Retrieved March 5, 2014 from http://womensordination.org/blog/2014/03/05/base-communities-and-the-invisible/

Cott, J. (2013). *Susan Sontag: The complete Rolling Stone interview.* New Haven: Yale University Press.

Crocker, H. W. III. (2001). *Triumph: The power and the glory of the Catholic Church, A 2,000-year history.* Roseville, California: Prima Publishing.

De Lubac, H. (1967). *The religion of Teilhard de Chardin.* (R. Hague, *Trans.*) New York: Desclee Company

Emmerich, A. C. (2005). *Mary Magdalen in the visions of Anne Catherine Emmerich 1774-1824.* Rockford, Illinois: Tan Books and Publishers, Inc.

Fiorenza, E. S. (1976) Women Apostles: The Testament of Scripture. In A. M. Gardiner (Ed.). *Women and Catholic priesthood: An expanded vision, Proceedings of the*

Detroit ordination conference. (pp. 94 – 102). New York: Paulist Press.

Fiorenza, E. S. (1983). *In memory of her: A feminist theological reconstruction of Christian origins.* New York: The Crossroad Publishing Company.

Follett, M. P. (1951). *Creative experience.* New York: Peter Smith.

Frugoni, C. (1992). The imagined woman. In G. Duby & M. Perrot (Eds.) *A history of women in the West*: Volume II. *Silences of the Middle Ages.* (pp. 336-422) Cambridge, Massachusetts: Belknap Press of Harvard University Press.

Gaudium et Spes: Pastoral constitution on the Church in the modern world. (1965). Promulgated by Pope Paul VI. Retrieved May 24, 2014 from http://www.vatican.va/archive/hist_councils/ii_vatican_c ouncil/documents/vat-ii_const_19651207_gaudium-et-spes_en.html

Gardner, E. (1908). St. Catherine of Siena. In The Catholic Encyclopedia. New York: Robert Appleton Company. Retrieved March 16, 2014 from New Advent: http://www.newadvent.org/cathen/03447a.htm

Gardner, E. G. (2009). *The road to Siena: The essential biography of St. Catherine.* Brewster, Massachusetts: Paraclete Press.

Groppe, E. (2009). Women and the persona of Christ: Ordination in the Roman Catholic Church. In Abraham, S. & Procario-Foley, E. (Eds.) *Frontiers in Catholic feminist theology: Shoulder to shoulder.* (pp. 153-171), Minneapolis: Fortress Press.

Halter, D. (2004). *The Papal no: A comprehensive guide to the Vatican's rejection of women's ordination.* New York: The Crossroad Publishing Company.

Henold, M.J. (2008). *Catholic and feminist: The surprising history of the American Catholic feminist movement.* Chapel Hill, North Carolina: The University of North Carolina Press.

Hinsdale, M. A. (2006). *Women shaping theology: 2004 Madeleva lecture in spirituality.* New York: Paulist Press.

Hinsdale, M.A. (2011). *St. Mary of Magdala: Ecclesiological provocations.* Catholic Theological Society of America: Proceedings Vol. 66 (2011) (pp. 67-90) Retrieved March 6, 2014 from http://ejournals.bc.edu/ojs/index.php/ctsa/article/view/5024

Kienzle, B. M. (1998). The Prostitute-Preacher: Patterns of Polemic against Medieval Waldensian Women Preachers. In B. M. Kienzle & P. J. Walker (Eds.) *Women preachers and prophets through two millennia of Christianity.* (pp. 99-113) Berkeley: University of California Press.

Kirsch, Johann Peter. "St. Euphrosyne." The Catholic Encyclopedia. Vol. 5. New York: Robert Appleton Company, 1909. 6 Jun. 2014 <http://www.newadvent.org/cathen/05606c.htm>.

Lumen Gentium: On the Church. (2013). *The Second Vatican Council: The Four Constitutions.* (Trans. Catholic Truth Society). San Francisco: Ignatius Press.

Maslow, A. H. (1971). *The farther reaches of human nature.* New York: The Viking Press.

Meir, G. (1975). *My life.* New York: G.P. Putnam's Sons.

New American Bible (2011). Charlotte, North Carolina: Saint Benedict Press, LLC

Noonan, J.T. Jr. (2005). *A church that can and cannot change: The development of Catholic moral teaching.* Notre Dame, Indiana: University of Notre Dame Press.

O'Neil, L. (2014, February 24). *Catholicism, Women + the Winds of Change.* Ozy Online. Retrieved February 28, 2014 from http://www.ozy.com/fast-forward/catholicism-women-the-winds-of-change/6548.article

Ott, M. (1909). Pope Gregory XI. In The Catholic Encyclopedia. New York: Robert Appleton Company. Retrieved March 31, 2014 from New Advent: http://www.newadvent.org/cathen/06799a.htm

Padberg, J. W. S.J. (Ed.) (2009). *Jesuit life & mission today:* The decrees of the 31st-35th general congregation of the Society of Jesus. Saint Louis: The Institute of Jesuit Sources.

Pentin, E. (2014, April 3). The Pan-Orthodox Council, Ukraine Crisis and Christian Unity: An interview with Metropolitan Hilarion Alfeyev of Volokolamsk, the chairman of the Russian Orthodox Department of External

Church Relations. *The National Catholic Register*. Retrieved May, 5, 2014 from http://www.ncregister.com/daily-news/the-pan-orthodox-council-ukraine-crisis-and-christian-unity/

Pew Research Center. (2013, March 13-17). National Survey. Retrieved November 19, 2013 from http://www.pewforum.org/2013/03/18/us-catholics-happy-with-selection-of-pope-francis/

Pontifical Council for Culture (2003). *Jesus Christ, The Bearer of the Water of Life*. Retrieved March 8, 2014 from http://www.vatican.va/roman_curia/pontifical_councils/interelg/documents/rc_pc_interelg_doc_20030203_new-age_en.html

Pope Emeritus Benedict. (2000). *The spirit of the liturgy*. (J. Saward. *Trans.*) San Francisco: Ignatius Press.

Pope Emeritus Benedict (2004) *Introduction to Christianity*. (J.R. Foster, *Trans.*) San Francisco: Communio Books, Ignatius Press.

Pope Nicholas V. (1455, January 8). *Bull Romanus Pontifex*. Retrieved November 25, 2013 from http://en.wikipedia.org/wiki/Romanus_Pontifex

Rahner, K. *The content of faith: The best of Karl Rahner's theological writings*. (Eds. K. Lehmann & A. Raffelt). (*Trans.* H. D. Egan, S.J.).

Ruether, R. R. (1976). Ordination: What is the Problem?. In A. M. Gardiner (Ed.). *Women and Catholic priesthood: An expanded vision, Proceedings of the Detroit ordination conference*. (pp. 30 – 34). New York: Paulist Press.

Ruether, R.R. (1993). *Sexism and God-talk: Toward a feminist theology*. Boston: Beacon Press.

Ruether, R. R. (2005). *Goddesses and the divine feminine*: *A western religious history*. Berkeley: University of California Press.

Soloviev, V. (2013). *Russia and the universal church*. Chattanooga: Catholic Resources.

St. Catherine. (1980). *Catherine of Siena: The dialogue*. (Noffke, S. Trans.) New York: Paulist Press.

Swidler, L, & Swidler, A. (1977). (Eds.) *Women Priests: A Catholic Commentary on the Vatican Declaration*. Paulist Press. The book is available online at http://www.womenpriests.org/classic/wp_cont.asp

Trasancos, S. (2013). *Science Was Born of Christianity: The Teaching of Fr. Stanley L. Jaki*. Kindle Edition. Retrieved March 13, 2014 from http://www.amazon.com/gp/product/B00H3T59XE/ref= oh_d__000_details_000__i00?ie=UTF8&psc=1

Undset, S. (2009). *Catherine of Siena*. (K.A. Lund, *Trans.*) San Francisco: Ignatius Press.

Vatican Information Service. (2014 March 10). *Angelus: Do not enter into dialogue with Satan—only God's word will save us*. Retrieved March 10, 2014 from http://www.visnews-en.blogspot.com/2014/03/angelus-do-not-enter-into-dialogue-with.html

Vecchio, S. (1992). The good wife. In G. Duby & M. Perrot (Eds.) *A history of women in the West*: Volume II. *Silences of the Middle Ages*. (pp. 105-135) Cambridge, Massachusetts: Belknap Press of Harvard University Press.

About the Author

David H. Lukenbill is a former criminal—thief and robber—who has transformed his life through education—an Associate of Arts degree in Administration of Justice from Sacramento City College, a Bachelor of Science degree in Organizational Behavior from the University of San Francisco, and a Master of Public Administration degree from the University of San Francisco—several years developing, managing, and consulting with criminal transformative organizations, a conversion to Catholicism and a strong marriage and family life.

He is married to his wife of 31 years and they have one child. They live by the American River in California with two cats, and all the wild critters they can feed.

Contact information

David H. Lukenbill, President
The Lampstand Foundation
Post Office Box 254794
Sacramento, CA 95865-4794
Email: Dlukenbill@msn.com

Prayer for Prisoners, Pope Pius XII

O **Divine Prisoner** of the sanctuary, Who for love of us and for our salvation not only enclosed Yourself within the narrow confines of human nature and then hid Yourself under the veils of the Sacramental Species, but also continually live in the tabernacle! Hear our prayer which rises to You from within these walls and which longs to express to You our affection, our sorrow, and the great need we have of You in our tribulations - above all, in the loss of freedom which so distresses us.

For some of us, there is probably a voice in the depths of conscience which says we are not guilty; that only a tragic judicial error has led us to this prison. In this case, we will draw comfort from remembering that You, the most August of all victims, were also condemned despite Your innocence.

Or perhaps, instead, we must lower our eyes to conceal our blush of shame, and beat our breast. But, even so, we also have the remedy of throwing ourselves into Your arms, certain that You understand all errors, forgive all sins, and generously restore Your grace to him who turns to You in repentance.

And finally, there are those among us who have succumbed to sin so often through the course of our earthly lives that even the best among men mistrust us, and we ourselves hardly know how to set out on the new road of regeneration. But despite all this, in the most hidden corner of our soul a voice of trust and comfort whispers Your words, promising us the help of Your light and Your grace if we want to return to what is good.

May we, o Lord, never forget that the day of trial is an opportune time for purifying the spirit, practicing the highest virtues, and acquiring the greatest merits. Let not our afflicted hearts be affected by that disgust which dries up everything, or by that distrust which leaves no room for brotherly sentiments and which prepared the road for bad counsel. May we always remember that, in depriving us of the freedom of our bodies, no one has been able to deprive us of freedom of the soul, which during the long hours of our solitude can rise to You to know You better and love You more each day.

Grant, o Divine Savior, help and resignation to the dear ones who mourn our absence. Grant peace and quiet to this world which has rejected us but which we love and to which we promise our co-operation as good citizens for the future.

Grant that our sorrows may be a salutary example to many souls and that they may thus be protected against the dangers of following our path. But above all, grant us the grace of believing firmly in You, of filially hoping in You, and of loving You: Who, with the Father and the Holy Spirit, live and reign forever and ever. Amen.

O Sacred Heart of Jesus, make us love Thee more and more!
Our Lady of Hope, pray for us!
Saint Dismas, the Good Thief, pray for us!

Pius XII, April 1958

Prayer to St. Dismas

Glorious Saint Dismas, you alone of all the great Penitent Saints were directly canonized by Christ Himself; you were assured of a place in Heaven with Him "*this day*" because of the sincere confession of your sins to Him in the tribunal of Calvary and your true sorrow for them as you hung beside Him in that open confessional; you who by your love and repentance did open the Heart of Jesus in mercy and forgiveness even before the centurion's spear tore it asunder; you whose face was closer to that of Jesus in His last agony, to offer Him a word of comfort, closer even than that of His Beloved Mother, Mary; you who knew so well how to pray, teach me the words to say to Him to gain pardon and the grace of perseverance; and you who are so close to Him now in Heaven, as you were during His last moments on earth, pray to Him for me that I shall never again desert Him, but that at the close of my life I may hear from Him the words He addressed to you: "This day thou shalt be with Me in Paradise." Amen.

Prayer to St. Michael for Protection of the Catholic Church and Her Members

℣ **Glorious St. Michael,** Guardian and Defender of the Church of Jesus Christ, come to the assistance of the Church, against which the powers of Hell are unchained. Guard with thy special care her august visible head, and obtain for him and for us that the hour of triumph may speedily arrive.

℣ **Glorious Archangel St. Michael,** watch over us during life, defend us against the assaults of the demon, assist us especially at the hour of death, obtain for us a favorable judgment and the happiness of beholding God face to face for endless ages. Amen